MW01601514

The First 80 Years

An Embarrassingly Egocentric Autobiography

CLAUDE PAINTER

The First 80 Years
An Embarrassingly Egocentric Autobiography

Library of Congress
ISBN 978-0-578-78349-9
Printed in the USA
DP&M of Florida, LLC
511 E. Church Street
Jacksonville, FL 32202

Preface

I must acknowledge and thank Chris Dorman, my wonderful friend who allowed me to read a chapter of his autobiography-in-the-making and thus motivated me to write an autobiography of my own.

Thanks is due to a number of others, only a few of whom I can mention on this page. First among you is Esther, my wonderful wife of over 50 years who has a special gift of patience which she freely bestows on me and without which I would never have brought this book to a successful completion.

I will be forever grateful to Deanne and Brian Roes, my loving daughter and her husband, who surprised me at my eightieth birthday party with the first published hardcopy of this book. I had never expected to see it go beyond the home-printer and notebook-binder stage. Thank you for expanding this project into an official thing, complete with the formality of a library of congress number.

For additional encouragement and proof-reading assistance from my other offspring and their spouses, Eric and Anya Painter, Joshua and Donita Manning, I am indebted to you.

So many others played encouraging and supportive roles and sometimes are actually part of the story. My sincerest thanks to each one of you.

Claude
Email (claude@startmail.com), or message at Facebook or Telegram:

Contents

Part 1 - Autobiography   Page   1

The time has come to appease those who have urged me for years to explain myself. It was my hope to postpone that effort until reaching the century mark or to write at least from an octogeneric perch, but they would have none of it. So here goes.

Part 2 - Anthology   Page 177

Across the years I have been occasionally inspired or required to produce a composition of some sort which upon completion I felt inclined to preserve. In response to a suggestion that this book include some poems and other stories from the past, I have compiled an anthology of poetry and prose for inclusion here in my new repository, my new sanctuary of choice for such items. I hope you will relish rummaging 'round the repository.

Part 3 - Album   Page 235

It was requested that the book also include a collection of pictures, and that explains the album of sorts that closes out the book. That album was a bit of a challenge, as quality photos of days long gone are a rarity. But I pulled some together from old stacks or albums, photographed the photos, tried to improve their appearance with a bit of photoshopping, collected electronic pictures from anyone who could supply them, and here you have 'em, complete with explanatory notes and an ancestral chart allowing you to locate certain of my relatives in the pedigree. I did not include the picture of Esther sleeping over her computer. (Or of me sleeping over mine.)

Part 1. The Autobiography

The Farm in the North Woods

Mom and Dad were born and grew up in the deep dark woods of northern Michigan; Mom a few miles to the left of Hillman, a rustic little village on the Thunder Bay River, and Dad on a dairy farm a few miles north of the same little village. Carol was the last of nine siblings and "Jimmy", the seventh of nine.

Carol Hunt and her numerous older siblings grew up in a small house quite distant from a gravel road which bears the family name. Hunt Road is still a gravel road today and the same sandy lane still plunges from its shoulder, passing the mailbox, parting the brush and the trees for half a mile until it circles the crumbling silo and ascends into a clearing, home for more than a century to a little farm that my grandfather so laboriously wrested from the northern forest.

Carol graduated from Hillman High School and continued for a year of "Normal" school, as was required for a Michigan teacher's license in 1930. She then taught for a year in a one-room school house before the daughter of the schoolboard president, a year younger, also completed Normal school and assumed responsibility for the little schoolhouse. Michigan politics was no different a century ago.

Carol's mother was bedridden when my parents were married, so they exchanged their wedding vows in her Mother's bedroom. It was January 15, 1940, Carol's 28th birthday. "Jimmy" was almost 32.

Grandma Hunt

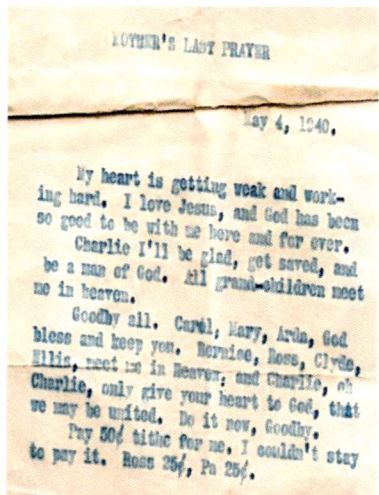

MOTHER'S LAST PRAYER

May 4, 1940.

Mother's Last Prayer—May 4, 1940

My heart is getting weak and working hard. I love Jesus, and God has been so good to be with me here and for ever.

Charlie I'll be glad, get saved and be a man of God. All grand children meet me in heaven.

Goodby all. Carol, Mary, Arda, God bless and keep you. Bernice, Ross, Clyde, Ellis, meet me in Heaven, and Charlie, oh Charlie, only give your heart to God, that we may be united. Do it now, Goodby.

Pay 50¢ tithe for me. I couldn't stay to pay it. Ross 25¢, Pa 25¢.

Jimmy was one of four sons growing up on a large farm. It was the responsibility of the boys in the '20s and '30s to help the patriarch with the farming, not to attend school and Dad would occasionally talk about his days as a boy plowing the fields behind a team of horses. His education was limited to a few months between harvest and spring planting, and even at that, he was not able to attend beyond fourth grade. As a result, his childhood dream of becoming a doctor was beyond unattainable.

My parents took up residence in a tiny four room house on Grandpa Painter's farm, north of town. Both of Jimmy's parents by this time were near invalid and all the siblings had married or otherwise flown the coop, so it was up to Dad to operate the farm single handedly, as well as to take care of his parents.

I was born nine months after the wedding on October 14, 1940. I came to realize later, and with justifiable pride, that I was born on Dwight David Eisenhower's birthday. Once Dwight and I actually exchanged birthday greetings by mail, as I was closing in on my teens and he was closing in on a second term as president. But I digress – and no doubt will do so again.

Somewhere within a few miles of Hillman was a junction where a country lane left the sandy sideroad, stole beneath a rustic log gate

and wound its way through the tall pines to a little home-built cabin nestled deep in the dark woods. It was in the little cabin at the end of that winding lane that I began the

Former Hillman, Mi. Free Methodist Church

journey of my life. Mom had a long and difficult first delivery which was great cause for concern to the midwife. But all's well that begins well. I am relating these details as they were related to me, the fact being that I personally remember little to nothing about the occasion.

3

After a period of recovery, we returned home to the four room house on the farm. The fourth room, the little one at the top of the stairs, became my room. I recall Mom relating how on the cold Michigan winter nights the wind blowing through the cracks in the walls would paste the curtains to the ceiling. We Michiganders in the '40s were a tough lot.

I claim only one recollection of my own, of those early days in the little farmhouse, and a traumatic one it was. For whatever reason, I was left alone in the house for a period of time, probably a much shorter period than it seemed. I awoke from a nap and heard Dad on the tractor, working in the field that bordered the house. That tractor went back and forth seemingly for days, Mom was nowhere to be summoned, and I thought I would die. Obviously, I thought wrong.

Dad's parents and siblings attended a Free Methodist Church in Hillman, a one room wooden structure with a wood-burning stove in the middle. I am not clear on how committed they were, but I think not very. For most of them, religion just didn't take. They lived hard and died young.

Lifelong cousins and buddies, Howard Rensberry and Claude Painter.

Dad was the fortunate one as he married wisely and spent his life with a woman who by her influence made all the difference in his life and the lives of his offspring. Mom was only a girl when a travelling preacher, a Free Methodist evangelist, came to Hillman to preach on the streets of the village. He procured use of the one room school house where Mom attended school in the woods west of Hillman, and he held several weeks of services there. Mom with her mother and siblings attended those services and came to know the Lord.

As a result of those meetings in the schoolhouse and the many changed lives which resulted, the Pleasant Valley Free Methodist Church was built in that remote area of the north woods.

Jimmy and Carol were married by Reverend Euler, (pronounced "Eye-ler."), the pastor of the Free Methodist Church in Hillman, which they attended until moving south in the state, and no matter where they lived from that time on, always they continued faithfully as members of the denomination.

I was to learn later of my many relatives, my cousins by the dozens who lived within fifteen miles of Hillman, but I have no recollection of them from these early years. I do have one picture of myself sitting on a toy behind a cousin, Howard Rensberry, with whom I became good friends as I was growing up and with whom I was a roommate for a year at Spring Arbor.

In 1943 Dad found a buyer for the farm and moved his young family, now including my sister, Lois, south to a farm near Flint in central Michigan. His parents came south also to live with their daughter in Oxford, Michigan. I have one faint recollection of visiting there, but the memory is not pleasant, as Grandad drooled all over the place and Grandma cried when we arrived and again when we departed.

Grandpa Painter died in 1944, a year following his move south, and was interred in a cemetery near where he had lived, north of Hillman. I recall attending his funeral in that old wood frame church in Hillman with the potbelly stove in the middle. That day in early Spring was blustery and altogether, too chilly; the building creaked and groaned as the wind blew it this way and that, and I was certain that we would all join Grandpa, interred beneath a pile of kindling wood. Fortunately, the building withstood the elements, living to creak and groan another day.

I have since visited Grandpa Painter's burial site. A large stone sits atop it, the inscription incomplete, as Grandma's side gives her name and birthdate, but displays only a dash where a final date belongs. I do not recall attending her funeral and my sense is that her daughters downstate found it more convenient and less expensive to burn than to bury. So ends the chapter of my grandparents and our life on Grandpa Painter's farm.

A Farm of His Own

Dad and Mom rented a farm near Flushing, Michigan. Farming was all Dad knew, so he did the obvious. I was three or so, and Lois was half my age. With help from the bank, Dad was able to purchase a herd of Holstein cattle, and began to farm for himself. It was an exciting time for him.

While living near Flushing, we attended the Free Methodist Church that sat on the front of the East Michigan Conference Grounds. I recall only one detail from our year at that church. The center section of the sanctuary had rather long pews with a divider in their middle. I suppose that was to hamstring kids such as I who were inclined to run around after the service. On one occasion a gentleman was standing next to that divider. We may have been singing or perhaps he was offering a testimony. But being the demonstrative sort as many FM'ers were in 1945, he suddenly gave a shout, went straight up in the air and came down on the other side of that divider. Now that caught my attention.

My few memories of that farm were, again and not surprisingly, mostly of traumatic experiences. The large farmhouse we lived in had a porch along two sides, perhaps even three sides. The railing had vertical rungs with enough space between to fit one's head. I recall a day when kneeling on the porch I looked over the edge, hanging onto a rung with each hand and pushing my head between. Then I discovered that I could not pull myself back onto the porch. Hanging head down, I shouted for help until it became clear that no help was within hearing. The only solution was to let go and tumble off the porch, landing on my head some distance below. We Michiganders in the 40's were a tough lot.

A small creek ran behind the barn down to the road, and disappeared under a bridge. It was fenced off to keep the cattle out. I recall the time when Uncle Ray, Dad's youngest brother, paid us a visit. We had a recent deluge which had swollen the creek to much more than its normal capacity. Uncle Ray saw opportunity to tease me a bit, and so threatened to climb over that fence. I could picture him being caught up in that current and swept away under the bridge never to be seen again. Beside myself, I pleaded with him not to climb the fence. Fortunately, he obliged, but I was scarred for life.

Dad's farming took a turn for the worse, as his herd of cattle became ill. The milk was not salable and had to be dumped. Of course, the cattle kept on eating, so had to be sold quickly. It was a sad morning when they were loaded on the truck and driven away. After a year on this first farm of his own, Dad was again out of the farming business.

Off to the Big City

Dad had yet another brother who lived in the Detroit area and had a business of his own. Uncle Clarence invited Dad to join him in working his business and again we moved. By now I was four, but still have few recollections about the year we lived in the town of Clawson, a suburb of Detroit. I guess I just didn't lead a very memorable life.

I do remember that our house was located near the end of a short dead end street. I remember watching a woman back her car out of the last driveway on the street. Unfortunately, she backed out the wrong way so that the car was headed toward the dead end. The woman thought for a moment before pulling into the driveway again. Again, she backed out and again faced the dead end. Even at the age of four I thought this was rather unusual behavior and more than a little humorous. Once more, the woman pulled into the driveway and on the third attempt found her way out of that dead end street.

We always entered our house in Clawson through the rear entry. There was a front door but the steps were missing, and it was a long way to the ground. Even so, Lois, my younger sister found it interesting to investigate that front door. Inevitably she would fall out and get hurt. After the third tumble out that door, Mom delivered a memorable spanking, and the problem was resolved. Actually, there may have been two spankings. I remember one occasion and this may have been it, when Lois reported that the first spanking didn't hurt.

Clearly, Lois was not the only one to receive a spanking during this time period. I have in my possession a letter written by Mom to her eldest sibling, my Aunt Arda, who still lived 250 miles north in the house where Mom and her eight brothers and sisters had grown up. My guess is that Aunt Arda received the letter about February of 1946, when I was a five-year-old kindergartner and Lois had just turned three. It reads as follows:

Dear Sister Arda,

I'm glad you received the Gum OK and sorry I haven't answered any letters nor sent any more gum but will as soon as possible. I'm not much of a letter writer any more just can't get the time to stop that long in the day. Can't take a nap and rest good either, my work haunts me if I try to sleep. But I have to get up at 5:30 or six so I don't get the rest I need. I sewed yesterday: at nite my feet and ankles were so swollen and stiff, didn't bend much. Jimmie is still working hard but its raining today so he's overhauling the car at Clarences. Children are asleep. We expect to take Claude to the hospital this month sometime if possible. He's not too well but eats pretty good at present. Gained ½ lb, since last September. Yes we realize I don't have patience nor kindness enough for Claude when I correct him. But as for love, he surely gets more every week than I can remember of getting at all. As a child I remember just one kiss that my mother gave me, and it surprised me. I remember just once that my dad held me – when mama was sick once, Claude gets from one to several stories read to him every day when he takes a nap, or at night. His dad plays and rolls on the floor with him almost every day or else they mourn, because he has been neglected. He always gets tucked in bed and kissed when he goes to bed. Rainy days we sit and make valentines, scrap books, horns, whistles, kites and so on. He's a great guy for cookies, and stands on a chair and watches every move. Has a rabbit and valentine cookie cutter. He has a disposition that we understand, and don't baby him much when he gets hurt, because once you start humoring him you've got your hands full. We don't allow him to get away with much, because children who get a habit deceiving, will no doubt deceive themselves out of heaven. We get some rebukes but we get quite a lot of compliments too, how nice our children act in church etc. I don't use the kindness (don't possess the grace) I realize it and it's a matter I'm much concerned about. Just last Sunday I testified to it, but when a 5 year old child rolls all over the coal pile with his best snow pants, after he has been warned, especially on Sat. nite when your car is broke and you have to take a bus to church, it's nothing to snicker about. We don't whip him much now as we realize his health is needing correction, but laws are of no use without the enforcement, either in the state or in the home.

We want him to be obedient and thrifty and I believe God

can use a child who has been over corrected more than one who has not received his correction. I don't want no spoiled baby that has to lean on his mama like Ross did. To my mind they are the most useless helpless fellows there are. We bought him 50 cents of valentines for his class at school. And last week made him some of the nicest pants, out of a man's suit! I designed a ship on it and, say, that nite in church he crossed his legs and folded his hands like a millionaire. After church he went and showed Brother Cross and Brother Yax and Sister Yax his new pants. Also the Sunday School Supt and his wife and about a half dozen more. Jimmie got him some new boots (overshoes) Saturday. So he made his rounds with them, too. Jimmie tells me I stick up for Claude and spoil him and neither Clarence nor Ray like the way I let him go and tell Jimmie off, very occasionally, but I like justice in all things and I don't want anyone teasing him, especially when he's not well.

When we go away from home we try not to let the children annoy anyone or be a nuisance. We don't have much time to spend on them and so naturally they get into more things to be scolded for, etc. That's hard on the children, too.

Sister Euler {pastor's wife,} didn't think you should speak quick to the babies. She gave her child law with no enforcement. And her Bro in law, (Rev. Schmidt), said he was the meanest child he ever saw. Bro. Euler's oldest sister said she surely feared for them if they didn't do something about him. And the next year the district elder took them in hand. Said they'd have to correct that child or else. And Sister Euler said, "it would be different if we weren't trying," but I dare say if we had given Claude the same training that her David got, we would have had something worse to contend with than they have. I've never left Claude with anyone because I know it takes an iron will to enforce what he is told to do. I, or we, want them to be a blessing to their parents and also the church because they've been made to do the right, while they are small. Another 5 or 6 years will almost be out of our reach, so I do feel we'll have to be stern with our responsibility. We got 11 eggs Saturday and have 15 hens. Pretty good.

Love,

Carol and family.

About six weeks prior to my fifth birthday, I began kindergarten in the Clawson school system and spent a number of months there. My only memory of that time was an afternoon when I fell asleep at my desk. Of course, I don't remember falling asleep but I do remember waking up. When the teacher brought me around, I was the only other one in the room, as the rest of the class had been dismissed for the day. I'm thinking the other kindergartners probably all tiptoed out of the room.

And Back to the Farm

It was March of my kindergarten school year when Dad decided enough of his brother, and again we moved, back to the Flint area to resume farming.

A couple of miles north of the village of Durand, between Flint and Lansing was a farm that Dad rented. Again, a herd of Holsteins, tractor and tools to work the ground, and again we were in business.

I found myself back in kindergarten to finish out the year, but the school was once again a one room school with eight grades and a potbelly... stove. Aha, you thought I was going to describe the teacher.

In the early spring of 1946 as we were now settling into our new home, the first Sunday rolled around and it was time to find our new church. The family piled into the old Chevy and rode into town. When Dad spotted an elderly gentleman walking down a village street, he pulled over to ask for directions to the Free Methodist Church. The response: "I'll take you there!" and he jumped into the back seat with us kids.

"Sam Hatt is my name," he told us upon our arrival, and then walked into church and sat down with us.

Turns out, he and the Mrs. had attended Durand Free Methodist for many years.

Sam and "Sister Hatt" became important people in my early memories of my church. I remember sitting while still at a tender age with Mom and others who surrounded the quilting frame that took up most of Sister Hatt's living room, and placing my stitches ever so carefully around the outlines on the quilt.

Many were the delicious dinners following a morning service that we enjoyed around Sam's table. Many were the admonitions from Sister Hatt: "Now Sam, don't get gravy on your tie!" You see, Sam loved gravy on his apple pie; a practice I never quite understood but it certainly worked for him.

Sam and the Mrs. are long gone, of course, but fondly remembered as one more window into a church that was so important in the life of a young farmer boy.

Being a young farmer boy surely had its risks, and in retrospect I think it was only by the quick reaction of my guardian angel that I even survived those days as a farmer boy. Although any number of stories could justify my thinking, one should be sufficient to make the point.

One summer day I was riding in the hopper of the combine as Dad, high on his tractor, pulled it around the field. As the bushels of wheat flowed like a golden stream into the grain hopper, slowly the level of wheat rose higher and higher until the hopper was filled to overflowing and there I sat, high atop the rounded load of wheat – and high above the ground. As Dad hit the brake, I suddenly pitched forward off the overflowing hopper, narrowly missing the whirling driveshaft between tractor and combine and landed flat on my back in the hay stubble between them. As Dad saw me hit the ground he jumped from his seat, releasing the brake pedal from beneath his foot and allowing tractor and combine to leap forward. Again, he hit the brake, by which time the tire bearing that hopper full of grain was pressing against the top of my head. Wonder of wonders, there were no injuries, I soon regained my breath, and that was my last ride on the combine.

On one occasion when I was about seven or eight years old, I accompanied my father on a drive to a neighboring farm. The front yard had a large circle drive from the gravel road, or more accurately a "U" shaped drive, with the entry point into the drive being at a higher elevation than the exit at the other end.

Dad parked the car at the base of that "U" where the decline in elevation occurred. He left me sitting in the front seat and peering through the windshield at a structure just ahead of the car. It was a tall metal framework painted bright red and supporting a very large tank of gasoline. A path was worn next to the structure where the farmer parked his tractor before roaring down the lane to go to work, and there, gravity would fill the tractor tank through a large hose hanging from the tank high atop the bright red frame.

As I sat there looking at that structure with the tank of gas looming above, I could almost imagine the car rolling down that incline, crashing into the structure and dropping that huge tank of gas onto the car. And then suddenly I realized I was not imagining. The car was indeed, rolling toward the structure.

I didn't know how to use those pedals on the floor, and couldn't reach them, anyway. But there was that big steering wheel. I grabbed that wheel and pulled with both hands, turning, slowly turning...

Of course, my father and his friend who were standing some distance away, could only watch in helpless disbelief as the car rolled down the incline, slowly veered from its path, squeaked by that structure with inches to spare and rolled to rest down near the barn. Needless to say, I was the hero of that day.

Unlike my father's childhood experience, when the school door opened for me, I was there to walk through it. For a year I trekked the half mile to and from the little schoolhouse with eight grades and a pot-bellied stove. It was during this year that my musical inclinations began to appear. After a few weeks of "music class" when the teacher gathered eight grades and kindergarten around the piano to sing "The Erie Canal," she sent a note home to Mom.

The teacher reported that there was an alto in her music class and eventually she ID'd him as the lone kindergartner.

One thing led to another and soon Mom and I were singing duets at communitywide church events in our town. I stood next to her on a chair behind the pulpit, and sang alto to accompany her soprano. It was something of a rush for this shy one from the north woods, and even at such a tender age I began to thrill to the attention. The downer was the part afterward when all the old ladies wanted to kiss me.

Music was to become an important element in my life. It was years later that I came to realize the significance of a contribution Grandma Hunt had made to her grandchildren's musical inclinations, even though she had passed before they were even born. From Grandma's meager estate Mom received fifty dollars which she saved and earmarked for the purchase of a piano. In time she was able to buy a used piano with a fifty dollar price tag, a player piano with a huge box of rolls, a monstrously heavy upright that greatly agitated Dad as we moved from place to place. But Lois and I were able to grow up with a piano always standing in our living room and it served us well when the time came for piano lessons. Thank you, Grandma Hunt.

Another Move

I finished out kindergarten at the country school, but since a new kindergartner was coming to school in the fall, and I was the only candidate for first grade, the teacher thought it expedient to leave me with the new kid for another year.

Fortunately for my school career when Dad's year-long lease on the farm expired, we moved to another larger farm near Bancroft, a neighboring village. No one-room schoolhouse this time. Our farm was at the edge of town and our new home with the beautiful stained glass windows in the parlor was just across the street from the school, an actual two-story brick building having only two grade levels per teacher. My new kindergarten teacher was not only, also the firstgrade teacher, but the principal as well. After my first few days in her class she wrote a note to Mom explaining that I was the best reader in her room and was being put into first grade. Another three months in her room and she passed me into second grade. I was back on schedule.

Now I was in the second and third grade room on the second floor of the brick building. Other than reading class (for which I always finished the newly distributed reader within a day or so), I was not especially smitten with school, but for cursive practice I reserved an especially high level of contempt, the result of which is obvious in my penmanship to this day.

When I could take it no longer, I would stand at that broad second story window staring out at the street and at my house on the other side until the teacher would tell me to retake my seat. One day I had a brilliant idea. Since the "boys' room" was on first floor, all I had to do was hold one finger in the air. Down the stairs and across the road I went, freed from the shackles of that institution.

Unfortunately, my mother was quite perceptive and my father quite pitiless. She "supposed" I must be sick and sent me to bed. He "supposed" I needed a strap on my seat, after which he returned me to school. Clearly, my teacher slash principal hadn't heard the rules about double jeopardy, evident by her own application of a board to my bum before returning me to the classroom. So utterly unfair.

The parlor with the beautiful windows became my bedroom because we really had no need for the second story nor for a parlor. However, on those frigid winter nights, the big double doors were opened and my bed was rolled out into the large dining room with the coal-burning stove, where I could stay toasty warm at minimal expense.

It was on the street between school and house and with the aid of a couple of neighbor kids that I first mounted a bicycle, one that was too large for my stubby legs, one which wobbled dangerously as I rode it down the hill.... Correction: ....as it rode me down the hill. I was really not in control. At the bottom I discovered that the bike was six inches too tall to allow for a dismount nor would it even stop that I might make the attempt. There was of course the option of turning around in a big shaky circle, but space was limited due to an enormous shiny Buick. What an inglorious impact!

Ah, the technology of the time. Here in Bancroft we had our first telephone. It hung on the wall docilly enough, crank at the ready, until a call came in to one of the phones on the ten-party circuit. Then the ringer with a level of decibels similar to the bells at a railroad crossing would tell the world with a long, a short and a long, or with three longs and a short, just which house on the street had an incoming. The person receiving the call could esti-mate the number of eavesdroppers on the line by the degree of fade in the signal.

For an outgoing call one had to crank the handle on the side of the phone, much as grandpa might have cranked up the old John Deere tractor. This would summon the operator so that you might give her a three digit number or simply the name of the friend you wished to contact. She would ask about the health of the family, perhaps comment on the day's weather and then plug you in to your party. So remarkably up-to-date we were in Bancroft.

As a young lad it was my responsibility to take the monthly pay-ment three blocks down the street to the phone building where on a hot day the operator sat with the door open. I would stand trans-fixed as she moved plugs from socket to socket in the big board full of holes that stood like a pokadot wall before her, talking to her customers as she worked until she had a moment to invite me in and receive my payment.

A New Home

March arrived in 1948 as it seemed to on an annual basis, and with it the annual expired rental contract and the annual move to the next supposedly better farm, this time on Brittain Road just south of Bancroft. Two details distinguished this move from the previous ones: We remained here for two entire years, and they were to become my final two years as a farmer boy. I was now seven and a half and in second grade. For the first time I can say the memories are numerous and vivid.

Our new home was a large two story red brick house with a large coal burning furnace in a large basement. The furnace discharged its heat through a grate, perhaps thirty inches square, in the central room of the first floor. Above that grate was a smaller one in the ceiling through which heat could rise into the second floor, but since we never used the numerous bedrooms above, the upper grate was always closed. This also prevented second-story wasps from violating our airspace.

I was always intrigued by the huge hole lined with sheet metal below that first floor grate and so on one occasion I decided to investigate. I managed to pick up the grate, no little feat, mind you, but I miscalculated that first step away from the hole, stepping instead, wouldn't you know, into the hole. Down I went into the sheet metal box, bruising my side badly as I scraped down the edge of that opening. The grate crashed to the floor and Mom came on the run to see what on earth was happening. My investigation now complete, I never again lifted the grate from that hole.

The dining room, living room and parlor were in one long row from back to front of the house, the parlor looking out on the lonely gravel road passing by. Once again, the parlor became the kids' room. My parents' bedroom sat off the side of the living room, the kitchen to the side of the dining room with its outer door leading down the porch steps and to the barnyard.

Those three main rooms were connected by large double doorways. Hinged doors hung between living room and parlor. But the opening between living room and dining room was another story. It was crowned with the most beautiful arch of intricate cherry woodwork rising for more than a foot above the doorway, row upon concentric row of little cherry trapezoids replicating the contour of the arch and all fitted together with astonishing precision. What gifted artisan in the 1800s would have created such beauty in an isolated brick farmhouse sitting on a lonely country road in southern Michigan?

Off the back side of the dining room was a little room, probably once a pantry but now a bathroom having even a bathtub. Based on prior experience I supposed baths were taken in a large circular galvanized tub which sat on the kitchen floor.

The red brick house was surrounded by a "lawn" which was mowed annually on the third of July, by the hay mower. Several small ramshackle outbuildings sat around the side or back of the house which in theory were the garage, the corncrib, the granary, the chicken coop and so forth. In most cases they were filled with boxes of miscellaneous rusty hardware which I repeatedly searched for parts needed to assemble picnic tables, ferris wheels and suchlike. Many were the flat tires on the family car as a result of nails and etcetera spilled in the gravel driveway, my construction site of choice. The ferris wheel, I must report never saw the light of day as there just were not enough suitable components in the boxes. Another story was the picnic table, kid size of course, for which I traveled down the lane to the woods, cut down some moderately sized logs and dragged them to the driveway for assembly.

One of those buildings had a second story "floor" made of large planks, perhaps "two by tens" which were quite long and distributed rather randomly across the joists. This was something else which required some investigation. All was fine until I stepped on the end of a plank, the other end went up in the air, I went down to the ground below. The plank standing on end followed me down, caught my shirt and pinned me to the ground, but remarkably never touched my person. I called for help without a response but eventually got my clothes loose from the plank and so continued with the day's activities.

Directly behind the house was the concrete block milk house where ten-gallon cans of milk sat in a big tank of refrigerated water. A rather large barnyard separated the milk house from the barn, so that morning and night, Dad crossed it repeatedly, often through snowbanks, often through mud that would nearly suck one's boots off, carrying two large buckets of that frothy white treasure and pouring it through a strainer into those milk cans.

There the milk would chill until the big truck from the dairy made its rounds. I used to marvel at the power of that muscular truck driver with the big leather apron as he pulled a dozen of those ten gallon cans of milk out of the water, hoisted them high up onto the bed of the refrigerated truck and then drove away to repeat the process at the next dairy farm down the road.

It was during this period of my life that my entrepreneurial inclinations began to float to the surface. Somewhere I found an ad for Cloverine Brand Salve which one could buy in wholesale quantities of ten or a dozen 1-ounce tins and resell them at a quarter apiece realizing a tidy little profit for one's efforts. Actually the ad was slanted toward the parent who would buy the tins, commission his kid to sell the tins, and pocket the quarters brought home by the young recruit. That doesn't sound fair unless one sees the ad showing the many marvelous toys which could be purchased with points earned by the under-age salesperson. I prevailed upon Mom to order a quantity of tins for me.

It was 1967, 20 years later, that the Federal Trade Commission poured cold water on this method of raising up a sales staff. However, if one is still interested in Cloverine Brand Salve, it is still available on-line from Walmart or Amazon; a three-pac for $15 or more, plus shipping.

In the fullness of time, seeming like 20 years later, the package arrived in the mail. I began my sales career at the neighbors' house across the road. An elderly couple who didn't have two nickels to rub together lived there. They invited me in and the gentleman interrogated me unmercifully about the quality and the value of my product. I finally had to admit that I wasn't sure whether Cloverine-Brand-Salve would heal the cracks in his barn. Even so, he went for a tin; I happily pocketed the quarter, said thanks and continued on my way down the road.

I had difficulty finding another farmer who could be sold on this product. I trudged the half mile west to the corner, turned left at the school house and continued south into uncharted terrain, stopping at every farmhouse along the way. A mile later I reached the next corner, made a left, continued on to the third left and the fourth, and a half mile later reached my home.

It is remarkable how hungry and tired an eight-year-old can become after walking around a square mile, and the experience resulted in a whole 'nother point of view regarding a career in sales. I have no idea what ever happened to those last nine tins of Cloverine-Brand-Salve, and just for the record, I didn't really care.

A New Barn

The barn was fairly large by local standards, with a bay in the middle, a "drive floor" through which a tractor and wagon might be driven or many tools stored during the winter months. On each side was a board wall about eight feet high and from the top of these walls a second-story floor extended to opposite ends of the barn. Flight paths of pigeons crisscrossed in the peak high above and it was in this enormous space between floor and flight path where baled hay was stored in the summer months to feed the hungry herd throughout the long cold winter months just ahead.

A ladder ascended the wall from the drive floor below, continuing by the upper floor and rising high into the stratosphere. When we first moved to this location, I would nimbly ascend into pigeon country near the peak of that barn. What a difference a year can make, as I came to realize how far it was to the drive floor below. Not for all the tea in China was I about to climb to the top of that barn again.

Near where the ladder passed the second floor, there was a hole about four feet square which opened through the floor of the hay mow and allowed bales of hay to be dropped into the manger area of the cow barn below.

From the perimeter of that square hole a shaft ascended toward the roof with the ladder from the drive floor continuing up the front side of the shaft. The shaft was open on the back side so that no matter how high the current supply of hay surrounding the shaft, there was access to the chute, to the shaft, allowing bales of hay to be dropped through to the concrete floor below.

27

Down below the hay mow (a word that rhymes with cow,) it was home for about twenty of those large magnificent Holstein milkers, heavy producers, with the occasional Guernsey cow mixed in to bump up the average butterfat a bit.

The milkers stood side by side, restrained, a long row of bovine heads poked through a long row of stanchions while they were being milked and fed, and for most of the time during the cold winter months while their pasture was beneath the snow.

Beneath the floor at the other end of the barn was another area with pens for calves and anything else which needed to be under a roof in the winter time. Dressed in my winter snowsuit I would sometimes go there while Dad was doing the chores and snuggle up next to a nice warm calf sleeping in the straw. It was so cozy.

Dad had a shotgun hanging in the barn which really was attractive to me. One day while he was safely at work, I took it off the hooks, and standing in the doorway, put it to my shoulder so that it pointed out into the barnyard. Nothing dangerous about that. After I pretended for a while, I placed it back on the hook. No harm had been done.

On the next day I repeated the procedure. This time, however, I experimented with the hammer as I stood in the doorway. I stood there for a time with the gun to my shoulder and pointing out the doorway. Suddenly there was a tremendous explosion and I found myself sitting on the floor. I sat for a moment, gun in my lap, wondering how I got down here. I had no memory of the kick of the gun or of being knocked backward. It was as though I was transported. First, I was standing, then I was sitting. Then I decided to be thankful that the cattle were all in the pasture, not the barnyard. At length I got up, removed the spent shell from the chamber and rehung the shotgun. I don't think anyone else was the wiser, but for sure, I was. It was some number of years before I again had my cheek against a gunstock.

I did have my responsibilities during chore time, especially in the winter when the cattle were confined to the barn. Our barn was not one of those high-falutin' barns equipped with drinking bowls at the sides of the stanchions, so my job was to move down the row of stanchions setting a five gallon bucket in front of each cow, holding a running hose in the bucket until the milker had drunk her fill of water, and then moving on to the next cow. Of course, that took a long stretch of time. I also dispensed a quantity of corn silage from the silo into the manger for each cow, gave each a scoop of grain on top, frosting on their bovine cake, and then followed up with hay, lots of hay in the manger.

It was also my job to climb the ladder to the haymow and throw the bales down the chute, that vertical shaft. On one occasion I dropped a number of bales down the shaft onto the concrete floor far below. The hay was still piled quite high in the mow, perhaps 25 feet above that concrete floor in front of the manger. As I finished my work, Dad shouted up the shaft to say that I needed one more bale. So that bale soon came down onto the pile – and I followed close behind. Since it was still in the dead of winter, there was still plenty of hay in the mow, all of which I had to descend through before I could reach the destination. Fortunately, those bales that preceded me kept me off the floor, but landing on them still took the wind out of my sails. I remember waking up in Dad's arms as he was running across the barnyard. He deposited me on the couch and returned quickly to the barn where the milking machine was still running.

During the summer months it was often my job to walk down the lane between the fields and bring the cows up from the pasture at milking time. It seemed perfectly normal as they would file in to put their heads through stanchions and wait to be locked in, but in retrospect it amazes me that twenty or more cows walk into a barn and go to exactly the same stanchion that they always get milked in. There is never a miss, never. How do they know? Can they count?

Also, I'm now wondering, how did I remember which cow belonged in which stanchion? Yet, I did. It is reassuring to know that, even at that tender age, I was as clever as the cattle.

I vividly remember the day those Holstein milkers got me into a peck of trouble. Dad happened to glance out the window of the house and discovered the herd milling about in the front yard and some of the cattle wandering down the road. He shouted at me to help get the cattle back into the barnyard. We did that without too much difficulty. The difficult part was to follow as dad pulled a whip from a nearby tree and I led him a couple of times around the house, feeling that whip on my legs the whole way.

It seems I had come through the barnyard gate and not closed it behind me. Anybody can make a mistake, yes? It was so unfair. But I never again forgot to close the gate.

There were a couple of pasture fields for the cattle when pasture was available. The cattle would browse first in one location for several days and then in another. In other fields that bordered the lane Dad raised alfalfa for baled hay in the winter, corn for silage and wheat to sell. Occasionally he would try something a bit different, such as a field of peas or soybeans or sugar beets.

In those days our Michigan fields were overrun with pheasants. And from experience I can say (in an understated manner of speaking,) it is most unsettling when one of those birds explodes into the air from the brush just in front of you. Even though you may know where that bird is hiding and what he will sound like when he takes wing, still he will startle the bejeebers out of you.

The Chinese Ringneck is a beautiful bird which made for wonderful hunting in the fall. It is sad that their numbers have dwindled so dramatically in the last 60 years due to the large farming operations and their elimination of fence rows and other favorable habitat for the birds.

The only downside to such a high population was the enormous pheasant appetites for certain field grains, particularly the soybeans which they simply loved. On many occasions as Dad was working with his big red Farmall model "H", pheasants would jump out of the weeds into the furrow he had just plowed and run along the furrow, just ahead of the tractor. Dad would pull a wrench from the toolbox beneath the seat and clobber a pheasant as it ran before him. He was a dead-eye with the wrench and it was not unusual on the next day to have a couple of tasty pheasants on our table.

A New School

When the school days arrived, once again there was a half mile trek back and forth to the one-room school house. Not so bad on some of those bitter cold winter days considering that some of the students had walks three times as long as mine. We all liked our teacher, and it was a nice cozy school with the usual pot-bellied stove in the center of the room. However, that "cozy" part no longer applied when one needed to visit the outdoor "restroom" behind the school.

For most of us I think the favorite class was recess. Often recesses were the longest class of the day, as no doubt the teacher needed to catch up on grading papers, and so on. Sometimes we had your normal recess time with softball games and such. More often the activities were more creative. We would build houses using brush for the structure and weaving grass thatching throughout the walls and roof. All was very warm and welcoming.

In winter some students would bring their skates to school as there was a creek nearby just right for skating. Building snowmen was a frequent activity, but the most fun was activity spearheaded by the big boys, digging forts and other types of "buildings" in the snow. This construction occurred a few hundred feet down the road where the wind-driven snow had been piled into deep ditches and crusted over, making it just right for excavation. Tunnels were dug inside those deep ditches, and big rooms, with here and there "air holes" opened through the roof allowing one to pop his head up to look around. This same kind of activity carried over in-to the spring time after all snow was gone, when the big boys excavated tunnels in the sides of the ditches. They got to be rather lengthy with a room or two along the way, but this activity ceased quite abruptly when the teacher got wind of what was going on.

I thought the best recesses were the ones in the fall, recesses during which the student whose farm was just across the corner would go home briefly to return with his little red wagon full of watermelon from the garden. Now that was a recess.

Naturally there were other subjects besides recess. Things like reading and arithmetic, but classes tended to be brief as might be expected when there was only one teacher to teach kindergarten through eighth grade. I was left with plenty of time on those chilly winter mornings to stand around the stove and soak up the warmth. I also had plenty of time to read books from the library. The library was a single bookcase sitting against one wall. I would go there often to look for a book that I hadn't already memorized. As time went on, such books became few and far between.

One day in my desperation, I picked up a book which I had always rejected before because it was so small, black, with fine print and no pictures. None! Not much of a book by my standards. But I sat down at my seat and began my first adventure with a classic, Treasure Island. It was incredible. I was riveted. I was forever changed. For two days I could hardly eat or sleep. That was the day I learned what reading is really all about.

This school and several other one room school houses in the county were part of a school district with the control center being the red brick school in Bancroft that I had previously attended. Annually the district had a "field day," an event at the red brick school which was attended by the students from the entire district. There were races and other competitions throughout the day, with a break for the lunches we brought from home. Being neither athletic nor competitive at that stage of my life, I mainly kept a low profile and awaited lunch time. That was the highwater mark of the day for me, as I had come with a dime, carefully guarded all morning, with which I was allowed to purchase a soft drink in a bottle. I had seen people drink a soft drink from a bottle but this was my first opportunity to do so, myself. I found it to be cold and tingly and oh so good.

A New Job for Dad

My father stood a bit taller than five feet, but not much. He was an incredibly hard worker, strong and tough as rocks. Finally, he was operating the kind of farm he had always wanted. The only problem was that it did not make a reasonable living for him and his family. He finally went looking for an additional source of income and found it in a small factory in Durand. Simplicity was the name of this little shop which built shakeouts, equipment used to separate stone from a gravel pit according to size.

Schedules were reset as now he rose at 4:00 AM to do the chores before driving the ten miles to his nine hour work day. Coming home, he would again do chores, get on the tractor, work the fields by headlights until coming in exhausted at 11 PM. After sleeping five hours, he would arise and do it all over again.

There were times when Mom did the chores. I don't know how she managed, but it allowed Dad to go straight to the fields upon his arrival home. I still remember seeing her limp around the barn with a broken toe. You see, one of the cows would not move over for her to hang the milk bucket underneath, so she gave it a good hard kick in the leg.

Sunday except for doing the chores, was a different day. All else was put on hold as Dad, faithful as sunup, would drive his family to Durand to attend church, not just once, but a second time in the evening. Only the vilest blizzard or ice storm would disrupt that routine and I have almost no memory of ever missing a service.

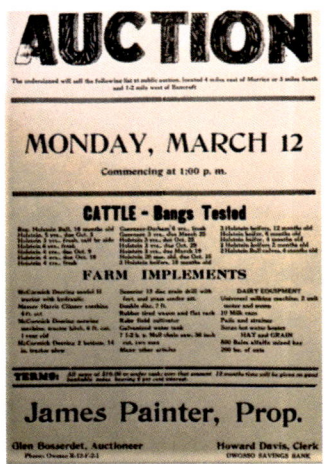

But the pace was telling, and with the end of the annual rent contract approaching, Dad sought relief from his unrelenting lifestyle and decided that farming was no longer the way to support a family. He had an auction to sell his cattle and farm equipment. Proceeds from the auction financed a down payment on a nice little bungalow in Durand.

As for the old farm south of Bancroft, I can become nostalgic about it without a lot of effort as I think back on those days before the auction. Such memories I hold, of the half-mile walks to school along the narrow gravel road, of stopping to play in the water flowing beneath the little bridges on the way, of the poison ivy growing around the mailbox post that added such interest to my summers, of the 4th of July observation on the front lawn, a slice in hand of the annual store-bought watermelon, of delivering up my solemn squeaky-voiced rendition of the national anthem to the fields of waving grain that surrounded me and defined my boyish world.

Seventy years later, the farmhouses are all gone, the barns that were scattered along the dusty roads, the one room school house with the thatched huts built by the big boys at recess time, the beautiful black and white Holstein milkers in the pastures, the fence lines where the elderberries grew tall and incredible numbers of pheasants raised their babies, the deer cavorting along the edge of the woodlot at the back of the property. Gone, it's all gone.

Only Britton Road remains, the narrow gravel track that I walked daily to second grade, and Scribner, the crossroad on which resided the school board president of those days for whom the road was named. Dusty roads they were, flanked by vast fields of waving wheat or rustling corn, their intersection marking the hallowed spot where I learned my multiplication tables and discovered Treasure Island and raised one finger or two to use the wasp-infested outhouse. Only a solitary pair of recently built houses now sit on the corner among a fleet of up-ended cylinders, fat metallic silos awaiting the ingathering, granaries raised to receive tons of golden produce reaped by bright red self-propelled harvesters crisscrossing the surrounding terrain.

Finally - Settling Down and Settling In

Once settled in the village of Durand, our days of moving every March were finally over. Soon, I began attending another red brick school house, this one being three stories high and my largest school since kindergarten near Detroit. Now nearing the end

309 Mackinaw Street, Durand, Michigan

of my fourth grade, I soon became good friends with my new classmate, Jim Williamson, the only boy in my class, ever, who was shorter than I was. Jim, however, was one tough young dude. A daredevil if ever there was one, who crossed rivers by crawling through the underside of bridge structures and who was usually successful in all sorts of remarkable achievements. Predictably, there were a few failures, and it follows predictably that he had experienced numerous broken bones and chipped teeth in his young body by the time I met him.

Jim had a personality so remarkably opposite my own reserved nature, and quickly became my protector as I found myself an easy target for the bullies in my class. I still recall the day when a pair of them ganged up on me as I was on my way home from school. Fortunately, Jim was near at hand and it was not long before both boys were flying down the street with Jim tight behind them. The direction taken by the bullies led them right by Jim's house and I can still hear his mother shouting through the screen door, "Jim! You leave those boys alone!" The chase now ended in a most inglorious manner, the fortunate duo continued to their homes, still on the run, and thanks to my new friend they thought twice before mixing with me again.

We still regularly attended the Free Methodist Church in Durand, and on one or two occasions I persuaded Jim to come to church with me. It made for a difficult morning, embarrassing at times, as Jim was a pretty uninhibited guy, not too concerned with Sunday School protocol or any other kind, for that matter. But we gave it our best shot. Interestingly I made contact with Jim after fifty years or so, found he was nearly recovered from a motorcycle accident that got him a thinking. He found his own way to church, turned his life around and become a died-in-the-wool Believer. I fully expect to see him on the Other Side.

There were a couple of elderly gentlemen who attended the Durand church, whose memory deserves at least honorable mention. Brother Cleveland was a retired minister; the Durand church having been his last pastorate. Upon his retirement, he bought a house and settled down in Durand, waiting for the last four or five of his numerous offspring to find a mate and move out of the house. Given enough time, most did that. I, for one, was sorry to see it happen because in the meantime, we always had plenty of "special music" in our services, women's trios and so forth, since the Cleveland offspring were all wonderful singers.

Brother Cleveland had moved past his own singing days but he could still pray and at considerable length. I must confess I took unfair advantage of that tendency. Our Sunday evening services always began with a thirty-minute segment conducted on a rotating basis by one of the "Young People" of the congregation. For "Young Peoples" as these segments were commonly termed, one of us would conduct a session of Bible Quizzing or of singing songs based on a specific theme, or of "sword drills," a friendly competition to see who could be the first to find and read a particular scripture reference. There were times, I confess, when I did not properly prepare, but I could always count on Brother Cleveland to pad the program for me if I called on him to pray.

Brother Ashford was another one of the truly faithful, never missing a Sunday evening service or Wednesday prayer meeting, even though he got no support from his wife. He did, however, have three sons about my own age who brought great joy into his life. I still remember some of the good times we had when they would come to visit on a Sunday afternoon. Visits to the farm were special for them, times when they could climb and swing on the ropes in the haymow. But even after we moved from the farm, they enjoyed those times at our place.

There was the time shortly after Christmas when they came for an afternoon and took great interest in a number of my nearly new Christmas presents. A favorite present that year was a new chemistry set that I had received. I had set it up very nicely on a table near the foot of the basement stairs. All the little bottles of chemicals, the Bunsen burner for bending glass tubing, everything was laid out beautifully. One of the Ashford boys was sitting alone in my basement laboratory and having the time of his life mixing chemicals and watching the result of his experiments. It seemed to be the perfect occasion to throw something down the stairs. Something like, oh, maybe a fire cracker.

Have you ever witnessed a twelve-year old having a heart attack? Howard was sure he had blown up the house. I recall that Howard's mother never invited me to spend time with the boys at her house. I could never understand that.

The school in Durand was the first I ever attended that had a real library. I loved that library, reading its offerings voraciously, visiting it on a daily basis to turn in yesterday's book and check out another.

I was perhaps fourteen when one day I was invited to the home of an elderly lady from our church, who had many books and who thought I might find some of interest to me. I was invited to help myself. What an afternoon I had going through the bookcases and boxes in her attic; I thought I'd died and gone to Heaven. I don't know what my dad thought when I brought those boxes of books home, but I'm sure Mom was delighted.

In seventh and eighth grades students were given a monthly paper, from Scholastic Magazine or somewhere, from which we could select inexpensive paperbacks that the teacher would order for us. What an exciting time when the teacher distributed that paper, and I went through, reading the blurbs and checking off all the "must have" books, doing my best to temper my appetite, knowing the wrath of my father that I would have to endure. He could not afford a box of paperbacks every month.

Of course, I put my order in first, so there was no going back. Then I explained to Dad that I really needed these 12 or 15 books, and they were very cheap adding up to only X number of dollars which I needed to have by next Monday. In the end, he always came through, and on the day when those books arrived, I knew it was worth it all. Thanks, Dad.

Our address was 309 Mackinaw Street. Dad bought the little two story in 1950 for the sum of six thousand dollars. It was 1100 square feet and was 40 years old when we moved there. Once more we were taking baths in a tub on the kitchen floor. That didn't last too long, thankfully, as Dad had an entire new bathroom installed in a little room off the back of the house.

The downstairs had a greater square footage than the upstairs so that my bedroom window looked out on the roof of the dining room below. It was very convenient on summer days to wake up early, climb out onto the roof and jump to the ground. I would then take a leisurely bicycle ride out into the country. I had my favorite places to walk into the woods or a cornfield that bordered, sit down for a time and watch the animals going about their morning duties. Fox squirrels were everywhere, big squirrels, not your mini grey squirrels that most have seen in the city park. Those ringnecked pheasants were everywhere. At times deer would advance to mere feet from me before snorting and plunging off through the corn. When I became sufficiently hungry, I would mount my bike and ride home for breakfast. Life was different at that time and place. Parents didn't worry much about a missing kid, at least not this kid. They knew I was enjoying myself somewhere and would return home when the tummy spoke.

Behind the house was an old horse barn, almost wide enough for two cars to enter, but not quite. It had a hay loft which made it a fairly tall building. One day Dad decided it was time to take the old barn down to make room for a real garage. I asked to be the demolition crew, and he agreed. The next morning, I began. I had a friend who began with me but quickly tired of the work. I continued alone and by evening of the second day it was flat on the ground. It took Dad considerably more time to get the lumber hauled away than it did to bring it down.

Farmall "H" - 1939-1953

Dad left the farm behind when he moved to town: the cattle, the fields, the farm equipment, all behind. All but the tractor. It was a number of years before he could sell that red Farmall.

Once settled into the new residence, he found some fields near the village which were for rent. He rented them, bought more equipment and begin tilling the fields, planting wheat or corn. I am sure the neighbors were amused when Dad would arrive home from work, to see him mount that red Farmall and go roaring down the streets, going off to work his fields.

Our only livestock, now that we were no longer on the farm, was the family cat. One day as I was mowing the lawn with our push mower, the old reel version as was common in the 1950's, that cat dashed across the lawn right in front of my mower, and his tail paid the price. After that day, the tail always hung strangely askew. Once a visitor came to the door of the house across the road. The cat happened to be on the neighbor's porch at that moment, and when the door was opened for the visitor, the cat trotted in, as though the house belonged to him. In doing so, he passed by the visitor who quickly reached down, intending to restrain the cat by his tail. He didn't slow the cat, not even a bit, but imagine his surprise as he now stood there, holding a cat's tail in his hand. According to the story I heard, he nearly passed out on the porch.

Two or three blocks from the house was the village park. During the summer vacation there were lots of activities offered there for the kids. A couple of times each week a bus or two from the school took a load of us to Meyers Lake where we could go swimming for a couple of hours.

A favorite activity of mine at the park was playing croquet. I became a master of the game. I was invincible. Eventually no one wanted to play when I was in the game. I would then offer to play partners, and select for myself a partner who was the absolute pits. Following the rules of course, I would drive my partner's ball as well as my own, through the hoops and we would still win.

45

On one occasion I observed a pair of ladies come to the park for a picnic. They found a picnic table, spread the table with things from their picnic basket: a table cloth, dishes, food and then sat down at the table. Both on the same side. The table tipped up and everything on it slid into their laps. So much for that picnic.

Dad eventually became bored with his work at the little factory, wanted to be his own man. He saw an opportunity to do that by taking on a gas station that was available for lease. Of course, a newly opened gas station is not immediately overwhelmed with customers. In fact, this one had only two or three customers per day. Dad was not one to sit still for extended periods of time and this station drove him into such a frenzy that he soon had to bail out of the arrangement. But having quit the job in the factory he was now without a source of income. He got a job on the railroad but that required days away from home, so that didn't last long, either. Eventually he applied and was rehired by the little factory in town. In time he did get his own business going, a septic tank and sewer cleaning business. Occasionally he would take on the job of installing a sewer line or septic system, subcontracting out the work. It was a tough job, sometimes requiring a jackhammer to open up frozen ground. But it was his own business at last, lucrative, successful, and he operated it happily until the day he sold it and retired.

As I grew into my teens, I also began making some money on the side. In summer I had a number of lawns to mow and in winter I shoveled driveways and sidewalks. Only once did I take on a job that was bigger than I could handle. After I had shoveled snow for hours, Dad came and helped me finish up the job. When summer rolled around, I was able to not only pay my way to camp but to send two or three others, as well.

As Christmas approached, I went door to door selling Christmas cards and taking orders for cards with names imprinted on them. It was a pretty lucrative business and I made enough to not only do my Christmas shopping but to buy a beautiful Remington semi-auto .22 caliber rifle. It went under the tree with MY name on its wrapping. It was to become my go-to weapon for collecting rabbits and fox squirrels for dinner and I still have and revere it to this day.

Durand was a friendly little town, population about 3000, strategically situated between Flint and Lansing, and central to Saginaw, Ann Arbor, Detroit, Grand Rapids, and thus this little burg became known as "the railroad hub of Michigan."

Durand Union Station / Michigan Railroad History Museum

Numerous rails entered the village from various directions and most any train if it was worth its whistle, passed through Durand. When one had to drive a car across our little town, it was an infrequent trip from point A to point B that didn't require a five-minute wait or perhaps a fifteen-minute wait behind the long gates with the bells ringing and the red lights flashing and a hundred boxcars slowly rumbling into or out of town. There were acres of railyards where long rows of boxcars sat until they were called into service. There was a roundhouse where steam engines went for maintenance and repairs. There was the Durand Union Station where passengers could mount or dismount from the passenger coaches. And of course, there was the noise. All day and all night, cars crashed against each other as they were hooked together, and were disengaged, changed engines or changed directions. Train whistles sounded and coal-fueled steam engines blew off their excess steam with a mighty whoosh-oosh-oosh. The local citizenry was oblivious to all this noise but overnight visitors to our homes were not oblivious and typically reported getting almost no sleep during their visit.

High School

There were two roads, Main Street and Saginaw Street which ran parallel through the village and were two blocks apart. The school sat between them and from them, cross streets ran diagonally to approach the four corners of the school. For years, Lois and I had a walk of about four blocks past the hospital where I lost my tonsils and appendix, across Saginaw Street and down the diagonal street in the picture to the three story red brick school building. Are all school buildings constructed of red brick? It seems to be the school-building material of choice in Michigan.

The school had a sort of tower at each end in which a wide set of stairs climbed to the second and third floors and then continued for another half flight to single rooms at the top of each tower. One room was the sound room from which announcements were broadcast and the Pledge of Allegiance was led.

I was in that room on only one occasion. It being D-Day, I was the one chosen to open the morning announcements by reading, "In Flanders Fields the poppies grow between the crosses row on row that mark our place, and in the sky the larks still bravely singing, fly scarce heard amidst the guns below…"

The room that topped the tower at the other end of the building was the principal's office, for many of us the most feared location in all the village. No one ever wished to be called into that room at the top of the tower. I was also in that room only once.

As I was walking down the hall peacefully and minding my own business, I met the principal walking in the other direction. Her name, the name by which students addressed her, was Miss Neal. But between ourselves, she was known by her first name. As Bertha passed me by, she said, "Claude, would you come to my office?" I responded, "Yes, ma'am," and she continued walking. In fear and trembling I followed her up the stairs, wondering where I had gone wrong. From behind her desk she invited me to have a seat. I sat down; she sat down in her big chair behind the desk. Then the question, "Claude, do you ever smile?"

That was not at all what I had expected to hear. Shocked, I stammered, "Well, I… I don't know. I mean… I never really… thought about it."

"Well," she said, "It is something you should think about. You may go."

What could I do? I took her advice and thought about it. I even tried to smile at people. It was very hard, but strangely, people began smiling back at me. That was a day when my life began to change. Thank you, Bertha; I have never forgotten the great kindness you did for me that day. It is right and proper that the next school building to go up in Durand was named the "Bertha Neal School."

Once in high school, I began to feel my oats. I think once I had begun to smile, I found how fun it was to make other people smile. My friend, Jim was no longer such a large part of my life and I still did not have many friends, but the ones I had were prizes. I can't explain why they tended to be a grade or two above me and in the "upper echelon" shall we say, of the student body. I suppose our common interests made the difference.

One was the son of the town's chief medical doctor, a man who was intimately familiar with my appendix. His driveway was heated so he never had to shovel snow. What a concept. Another friend, strangely enough, was a guy from the other side of the tracks, but that didn't get in his way. We all worked together on the yearbook, sometimes spending long hours to push it through the next deadline. These two were normally very involved in high school productions, the musicals and plays. I was their be-hind-the-scenes guy suggesting changes or slapstick additions that would cause the audience to dissolve into laughter. And best of all, they loved the screwy poetry I was often cranking out.

Too bad they graduated ahead of me and so never saw my favor-ite yearbook picture. We had about eighty kids in the choir which was problematic for the yearbook photographer. The solu-tion was to take two pictures as we stood on the risers, first the right half, then the other side, so we would come together for a two-page spread in the yearbook. Being the shortest bass in the choir, I always stood at the very end of the top row of guys. Once our picture was snapped, I ran behind the choir and jumped up on the top row of the tenor section for the next picture. Sure enough in that year's book I am smiling from the top row at both ends of the choir.

One of the janitors at the school was an elderly gentleman with whom I was well acquainted since he was a long-time attendee at my church. In tenth or eleventh grade, being the nerd that I was, I began following him around the school on his late afternoon and evening job, sweeping classrooms and halls, cleaning the stalls, taking the trash to the furnace in the basement. Soon I knew the ropes as well as he did.

One morning upon my arrival at school, I learned that Mr. Cleveland had suffered a heart attack and was fighting for life in the hospital. Folks in the superintendent's office were pretty concerned about who was to clean his half of the school that day. Seems, I was the only one who knew the job and so was requested to do an emergency fill-in for that evening. And the next. And the next.

The six or eight weeks that followed were positively exhilarating as I walked about the school carrying a ring of keys, had the responsibility of securing the building about ten or eleven each evening, and on pay day received the same check that Mr. Cleveland would have received had he still been on the job.

As for the downside, my homework suffered terribly, a detail which was eventually brought to the attention of the folks in the superintendent's office. It was inevitable. A replacement was finally located for me. I trained him for a few nights so that he could take on my job and my paycheck. I was left with the memory of all that authority, the appreciation of the office, a rather muted appreciation to be sure, but no matter - and a lot of homework to get caught up.

That used upright piano that Mom had purchased with Grandma Hunt's estate money now became a daily part of our lives as Lois and I began piano lessons. Our teacher was an elderly lady named Mrs. Belden who was also the choir director at school.

Mrs. Belden allowed me to join the A Cappella choir upon my entry into high school. She was desperate for tenors and supposed that at my tender age I could be of help in the tenor section. Matter of fact, when my voice changed it did not even pass GO! It went straight from alto to bass. In choir practice Mrs. Belden often caught me singing bass and reminded me that I was in the tenor section. But I couldn't handle those high notes. They hurt, Mrs. Belden!

One day after being caught again by the choir director, she said simply, "Claude, stop by the piano on your way out, today." Oh, I was in trouble, now. But wonder of wonders, Mrs. Belden had me sing a few scales and then said, "I think you belong in the bass section." But she didn't stop there. She asked, "Claude would you be interested in singing bass in a barbershop quartet?" What? Would

I be interested?

For the rest of my school days in Durand I was the little bass standing next to the superstars of the high school football team. The high point of my week was the practice session with the quartet as we perfected "I had a Dream, Dear," "Down by the Old Mill Stream," "My Little Margie," "Coney Island Babe," and many others of the barbershop genre. We sang at a variety of school events, became regulars on the local rubber chicken circuit, enjoyed free meals at church banquets. And the county-wide school competitions, what a blast they were. We stood in the lunch line with many students from schools across the county, choir members and band members often from schools much larger than ours. That was a favorite time of ours to suddenly break out in close harmony. Others in the line had not heard anything quite like this and would gather around us to take it in. Of course, hearing barbershop sung by a quartet with the shortest bass on record, that did nothing to diminish the novelty. Such chaos we caused with that lunch line. But all good things come to an end and I am happy to report, are often replaced with something even better. It happened in this fashion.

An Ambassador for Spring Arbor

One of the high points of my summer, (and there were many when I was a teen), was the time spent at our Free Methodist campground near Flint. This was the same campground having the church I attended when four years old; the one where the man leaped over the divider between the pews.

Annual camp and conference in our East Michigan Conference was a big deal and highly anticipated. There was a forty-acre camp site with many little cottages and lots of space *filled* with tents and trailers of campers from across the state. Camp meeting for the two largest districts, Flint and Lansing, was a week in length, and immediately followed by a week of conference when the current campers were joined by folks from the three other districts, Port Huron, Bay City and Alpena. As we lived in the Flint District, and only about twenty miles from the campground, we would set up a tent and move (refrigerator and all), to the camp ground for the entire two weeks. Dad could still work at his job during the day, and drive in to spend the overnight at camp.

For me, the high point of each service in the big tabernacle was a song or two rendered by a male quartet, four students from Spring Arbor College. Before each service there was a session with a volunteer choir practicing a song to be sung that evening. The quartet usually joined the choir for that practice and I always made it a point to capture the seat next to DeWayne, the bass from that quartet. He was the only base I ever knew, who had two capital letters in his name.

One evening during this practice he said to me, "Have you considered high school at Spring Arbor?" The school was at that time a two year institution but it also had a high school academy. I was about to enter my senior year. DeWayne insisted that I should ask my father about coming to SA for my last year of high school. I'm thinking, "This is ridiculous; like Dad is going to lay out all that money to send me away to high school." But I did as I was asked. Walking into the tent I explained about the Spring Arbor High School and DeWayne thought I should ask him about attending there this fall. Without a moment of thought, Dad replied, "Well, I don't see why not." You could have knocked me over with a feather.

Just like that, I left my barbershop quartet behind, and found myself in a third story dorm room at Spring Arbor. Within days I was accepted into the college A Capella choir, along with a few other high school students. Then I learned about tryouts to be held for a male quartet. This quartet would be scheduled to visit our denominational churches across the state to represent our school, as did the quartet I knew from camp. Of course, I tried out and was accepted into a new quartet composed of one other high school student and two college freshmen. Thus, the transition from barbershop to gospel music began. And when the next summer rolled around – and the one which followed – it was my own "Ambassador Quartet" making the rounds of our camps and conferences throughout Michigan, northern Ohio and Indiana. Not only was it great fun, it knocked half the tuition off my bill. And of course, I loved singing with these guys.

Spring Arbor Junior College and High School Academy was a pretty nifty little school in the late 1950's, having roughly 300 students in J.C. and perhaps half that number in high school, some of the finest of our denomination's young people in the Michigan, Ohio and Indiana area. We were a close-knit bunch of students with pretty much everyone knowing everyone else. We ate meals together, eight at a table, in the dining room which occupied the basement of the girls' dorm. Tables were set properly, we dressed neatly, serving dishes were passed clockwise around the table and every person ate what was served.

Friendships were built and memories accumulated, both of which lasted a lifetime. A favorite memory of mine, by way of example, is of a time when we had a short break from school, a great opportunity to go camping with a couple of my friends, Dave Parks and Howard Snyder.

It was mid-winter and very cold. We walked down to the lake which was a mile or so from school, and then continued across the lake on the thick ice. On the far side, we found some left over materials from someone's previous adventure, a couple pieces of tin and such, which were useful in building our little A-frame shelter. The snow was pushed out, some pine branches laid down beneath the sleeping bags, a roaring fire set blazing beneath a suspended soup pot and before the makeshift tent, and we were ready for the long weekend.

We went exploring the area, spent time inventing improvements to our camp site, and the highlight was the shooting of a fox squirrel with the little .22 rifle I had brought along. Once getting him skinned, (not an easy feat, I can assure you,) we cut a hole in the ice where we could clean and wash him, and then roasted him on a spit over the fire. Oh yes, he was quite tasty, although of a size hardly adequate to the appetites of three ravenous young men.

We slept well in our cozy sleeping bags, and arose with the sun to heat coffee over the fire and continue our adventuring. All in all, it was a great time, and one long remembered.

There was the year when the college scheduled a "special emphasis" week, a sort of spiritual retreat on campus, which coincided with a spiritual retreat of my own, the first week of the Michigan deer hunt. It had been my expectation to play hooky and join Dad in northern Michigan for the deer hunt. I asked but was denied special permission to follow through with my plans. That didn't make much difference to Dad, however, as he came down on schedule to pick me up, and phfutt! we were gone.

As it happened, I got a nice buck that year, my first one as a matter of fact, and I was the only one of my rather extensive party of relatives to get one. Somehow the news leaked back to school before my return. I got back just in time to join A Capella practice in session, and entering the classroom still in my scrufties, was welcomed with a resounding hand from the choir. That made it all worthwhile. I never heard a word from the administration about my absence.

The summer of 1958 was the first summer of the Ambassador Quartet. Oh, I know there were other summers with other Ambassador Quartets. Our name did seem to be a popular name for gospel quartets in those days. But this Ambassador Quartet was special because its members were Mark Mason, Ed Slater, Gordon Evoy and Claude Painter. Three of these gentlemen are now singing with the angels so it is left for me to relate the following untold story – again.

Our first gig was the rustic Alpena District Camp Meeting away up north in Michigan. Since we had a couple of weeks to kill between school and camp, we remained  on campus, employed in such enjoyable activities as painting stuff and cleaning ovens. "Someone" thought of a great idea. Why not ride bicycles to our first camp? It was only a bit more than two hundred miles and we had a week to make the trip. It was decided.

Of course, we didn't have bikes but no matter. There were a number of local individuals who did, and who loaned them to us. Old refrigerator shelves made great supports wired on the eight fenders. They needed to be well attached to support our sleeping bags and hammocks, our pots for cooking, our food, our clothing including suits for the week of camp. Two weeks of living was bundled up on eight refrigerator grates.

These bicycles, three of them anyway, were the old fashioned heavy sort with the wide rubber tires. We were to take turns riding those and the one new fangled bike having narrow wheels and a gear shift with three gears. Unfortunately, that gear shift was dysfunctional and required a full day of attention before it was finally made reliable. That day cut severely into our travel time; nonetheless we wanted to get on the road before the day was gone. At about 6:00 PM on a Monday night, our adventure began.

We biked about five miles before night fell and some rain fell with it. In the vicinity of – was it Parma? – we called it a day, found an old barn, and rolled out our sleeping bags in the hay. It was a long and chilly night, particularly for Ed who had the hammock. But we were on our way.

From that point the Ambassadors pedaled about fifty miles a day. However, we modified our modus operandi following that first chilly evening. Now we always managed to swing by a Free Methodist parsonage sometime in the late afternoon, and stop for a little visit with the pastor and family. "We're the Ambassadors, How d'you do, d'you do?" we would sing our little novelty song to them. Surprisingly they always invited us to join them for the evening meal. So, we would sing for our supper, supposing that to be the least we could do. Next would be an invitation to use the shower (big surprise...) and we would then be bedded down for the night. It was a brilliant plan and a no-fail system.

Up and at 'em the next morning. A solid breakfast and we were on the road. The roads we traveled were two lane roads, (not that there was much else in Michigan in 1958), and usually they did not have a lot of traffic to contend with. As we traveled farther north the land became quite hilly. Sometimes those hills seemed to go up forever but interestingly the other side seemed never to be nearly so long. It was then that this verse from Charles Tillman's song came to mind:

> *There are so many hills to climb upward,*
> *I often am longing for rest,*
> *But He who appoints me my pathway*
> *Knows just what is needful and best.*
> *I know in His Word He has promised*
> *That my strength, "It shall be as my day;"*
> *And the toils of the road will seem nothing,*
> *When I get to the end of the way.*

On one occasion we stopped for Cokes at a little Mom 'n' Pop store away out in the boonies. We stood around in the little building talking with the elderly Mom 'n' Pop tending the store, and then offered to sing them a song. Certainly, they didn't expect the sort of music they heard that day. Together they stood behind the counter weeping as we exhausted our repertoire.

By the end of the third full day – or was it the fourth – we had reached Rose City where thankfully there was a Free Methodist Church pastored at that time by "Sister Booth," a friendly former pastor of mine who was now widowed but still carrying on with her calling. Sister Booth gave us the usual treatment. I hope her pastorate added a little bonus to her paycheck in restoration of that which the locusts devoured as we passed through Rose City.

The next morning as we were about to set out on the final fifty miles of our adventure, we were greeted by a pickup truck and a car driven by cousins of mine who lived near our destination. They had heard that we were in the area and they came looking for us. It was in my considered opinion a rather inglorious conclusion to our great adventure as we loaded the bikes into the back of the pickup. But as we followed that narrow black ribbon up and down the hills and through the dark pines to our destination, it began to seem not such a bad idea after all.

The weekend ahead was great R&R following which we were able to climb the steps to the platform to sing on Monday night. I'm not so sure we could have done that two days earlier.

Dad with his pickup retrieved the four bikes and returned them to Spring Arbor. On my next visit there, I removed the refrigerator shelves and rode the bikes to their various owners. Well, let's say I rode three bikes to their various owners. But that skinny-wheeled bike that served so faithfully for two hundred miles, wouldn't you know: when I mounted that bike the gear shift broke.

Our normal form of transportation as we rode around the state was by station wagon; the old style nine-passenger sort, in which the rear seat faced the car traveling behind us. That seat was highly prized by each of us in the quartet, as the fortunate pair riding there was separated from the guys up front by a pile of luggage in the mid-section of the vehicle. Those in the back seat were inclined to leave the rear door open and ride with legs extended and feet resting on the tail-gate, a slice of watermelon in hand, a mouthful of seeds saved up to be blown at any car following too closely behind. One could do such things and frequently did, in 1958.

For three years I attended Spring Arbor, graduating from high school, class of '58 and junior college, class of '60. What a remarkable experience it was 60 years ago to attend this beautiful little school hidden away in a tiny village of southern Michigan, to graduate with a close-knit class of a hundred students, the cream, it is fair to say, of our denomination, students destined to become doctors and engineers, musicians and missionaries, authors and administrators, pastors and professors, many to become lifelong friends with whom I still remain in contact to this day. Sixty years later Spring Arbor Junior College and High School has become Spring Arbor University with impeccable credentials, numerous satellites and a student body numbering in the thousands. It never occurred to me when I lived and studied there, that one day I would have two children also attending and graduating from that superb institution.

In Defense of my Country

After graduation from Spring Arbor I returned home, expecting to find work over the summer and hopefully transfer to Roberts Wesleyan or Greenville, four-year Free Methodist schools in New York or Illinois. Things did not go well as I was unable to find any sort of a job.

The pastor of our church in Durand had a son who had graduated from Spring Arbor a year earlier, and returned home to work in a grocery store. He invited me on one occasion to accompany him to a neighboring town where he had an appointment with an Air Force recruiter. I told him, thanks anyway, Gordon, but I have no desire to talk with an Air Force recruiter. He cajoled me, said. "No, no, nothing like that, I just could use a bit of moral support as I meet my appointment." I relented and came along for the ride.

My friend had his conversation with the recruiter who then turned to me. He said, "You know, the Air Force has some very interesting career opportunities for anyone interested in learning a foreign language." How did he know linguistics was my weak spot? He continued, "You could study Russian, for example, and become competent in the language, use it on a dream assignment in Scotland or Japan..."

And I'm thinking, "That does sound pretty interesting. If I sit around here looking for work, I may just get drafted into the Army, anyway. Wouldn't that be the pits!"

The recruiter continued; "You could go in under the 'buddy plan' with your friend here. You would go through basic training together, conceivably continue on the same career path after basic."

For the second time that day, I caved in. "OK, Gordon, we'll go together. I'm going to study Russian."

What a fool I was. Two days later Gordon and I sat in a big room, blue with smoke from the cigarettes of nervous young men trying hard to grow up as they waited for their physicals. My turn came, I passed with flying colors and the next day was on an air conditioned train headed for Lackland Air Force Base in San Antonio. My 'buddy,' Gordon, flunked his physical and returned to the grocery store.

How did this happen? San Antonio in July, the doors of that air-conditioned train opened and I stepped out into heat that I had never before experienced. How did this happen?

Five foot six I was, a hundred twenty pounds, not an athletic bone in my body, surrounded by strangers, guys younger than me, bigger than me, taller than me, louder than me. Well, here we go.

Basic Training

We passed single-file through a room where men behind desks took a quick look, decided what size we were, and threw boots at us, uniforms, hats, underclothes. We came out the other side with arms full of new clothes. Our "civvies" were packed into a box and mailed home to mother. Our green fatigues had legs that were much too long. But we were given sewing kits and everyone sewed up his pant legs and cut off the excess. Well now I had an advantage over the rest of the guys who couldn't even thread a needle. I had sat for hours at the edge of a quilting frame.

As time went on, I discovered I could outlast most of the fellows as we ran around the track in the sweltering heat. Turns out, I held my own pretty well. I had a sense of humor and didn't hide it. And some of those big guys seemed to kinda like me. I was excused for a week from the normal routine so I could attend a language screening program, and the upshot of that was that I was recommended for Russian language school at Syracuse U. Things were looking up.

Until... One morning I sat my boots and my bunkmate's boots on the bunk while I swept underneath with the shoe brush. I had to hurry as the "flight" – as our barrack full of eighty recruits was called – had to be in formation on the street – very soon! I finished the job and ran to the street, got in line just in time. We marched off to our morning duties while the barracks was being inspected. We returned to find that both my bunk mate and I had been given five demerits. The boots were still sitting on the bunk. How did I forget to put them on the floor? Five demerits were no joke. Anyone who earned eight demerits throughout his entire basic training, would be sent to join an incoming flight and repeat his basic training a second time. Should he reach his limit of demerits on the second go-round, he would be discharged and sent home to Momma.

My first thought was for my bunk mate who now was awarded five demerits on my mistake. I couldn't let that stand. I approached the office of the "T.I.," the sergeant in charge of my flight. I knocked on the door and entered according to protocol. This sergeant was one tough dude. Walking into the principal's office was nothing. I explained to him that I was responsible for the shoes on the bed, and I requested that my bunkmate's demerits be given to me. The sergeant answered, "You know what that means." I responded, "Yes, Sir." He just stood there looking at me. Finally, he said, "Get outta here." And that was that.

We were only a week or so away from the end of basic. Our flight was in our dress uniforms and lined up at "Parade rest" out on the street. The sergeant stood in front and explained that when a flight completed its basic training, one man was selected for an award given and entered into his file as "the outstanding man of the flight." I stood there, remembering the various guys who came out ahead in the boxing matches or who had done really well when we ran bivouac... and suddenly the sergeant shouted out, "Painter!" I think only he and I knew why the smallest guy in the flight received that award.

Syracuse University

Following basic training, I enjoyed a short furlough at home and then it was off to Syracuse U. A disheartening pattern seemed to be developing as I had just spent the hottest summer months in South Texas, and now was to experience fall and winter in upstate New York. As it happened, the winter of '60-'61 was particularly bitter with one of the more ferocious blizzards on record. And after a Spring graduation from language school I would be back in Texas again, specifically San Angelo for additional school the next summer. Something was wrong with this picture.

There were many Air Force language students in one or another of the intensive language learning programs at Syracuse, but by far the largest number were learning Russian. We were stationed "on the hill," a location somewhat remote from either the main university campus or downtown Syracuse. Busses passed by our location however so it was easy enough to travel if we had time and inclination.

Our instructors were all native Russian speakers, and rather elderly. They all spoke English with a heavy accent and some with great difficulty, with one exception. One instructor was a gentleman who had studied English in London. He spoke impeccable Londonese with nary a trace of Russian accent.

In general, the job of the instructor was not to explain but to just conduct pattern practice based on sentence patterns and grammatical structures laid out in our books. We shifted hourly from one instructor to another, each session having a little different focus than the previous one. One daily session was actually a teaching session conducted by one of the instructors. We all came together for that session, a class on Russian grammar. The one thing I still remember from that class was a statement the teacher frequently made regarding a new word being introduced. As she wrote the word on the board, she would say, "This verd is a wurb."

This was for most of us a grueling nine months of school. There were instances in the program of suicides by those who couldn't make the grade or of feigned suicides by those who wished to be removed from the program. All of us had passed a test showing that we had an aptitude for language learning, although there were, shall we say some gifted persons and some extraordinarily gifted persons. Clearly and most unfortunately, I was not one of the latter. After our six hours in the classroom we studied or did homework for hours more in preparation for the next day. In my case I normally studied about six hours each evening.

In 1961 there was a new Walt Disney program on TV, a program of cartoons featuring the Roadrunner, Bugs Bunny and the whole assortment of characters. For many, that 30-minute escape from reality was the high point of the week, and the lounge with the tv was always filled to absolute capacity, with guys standing in the hall, straining to see through the doorway.

My escape was on Sunday when I would take the bus to the Free Methodist Church in Syracuse. I quickly made friends with a young married couple and with others there who would invite me home to a wonderful home cooked meal and return me to the hill before bed check. Soon others learned of my good fortune and began accompanying me to church. My new friends at church rose to the challenge and we all enjoyed good meals on Sunday.

Our menu on the hill left much to be desired. The dining room was not an Air Force mess hall in which the food would have been wonderful, but a university run cafeteria. No doubt food on the main campus would have been an improvement over what we were served, else, parents would have been transferring their freshman offspring to other universities. Sometimes as we passed through the serving line, a glob of something unidentifiable would be slapped onto our plate and would stick in place even when the plate was turned upside down. As a result, we tended to subsist on ice cream, lots and lots of ice cream.

Syracuse was roughly four hundred miles due east of my home in Michigan. Of course, a piece of Ontario, Canada dropped down between New York State and Michigan. A train ran almost directly between Syracuse and my home, crossing into Ontario at Niagara Falls. out again at Detroit and continuing west to Jackson, about 75 miles south of Durand.

The trip by train was about twelve hours in duration and often at night so one could sleep through much of it. It was not difficult to get home for Christmas and Easter break. At Christmas time Ralph accompanied me on that trip, since he didn't have much of a home to visit. Ralph was from Oklahoma and stood six feet six in his stocking feet. He was a young fellow trying to be grown up, with the cigars and all that stuff.

Ralph had never experienced a family or family life like ours. It was overwhelming to him. After a few days he asked if he could get an appointment to talk with our pastor, as he needed to find out what was going on. That was not difficult to arrange, and when Ralph returned from that appointment, he was a new and different Ralph. The change was so obvious and dramatic to his roommate when he returned to school that the roommate asked, what did we do to Ralph during that week? He had come home, promptly threw out all his tobacco, his pipes, his magazines. His speech was clean. There was a complete turnaround in his character. I lost track of him some years down the line, but not before meeting the woman he married, an attractive young lady, herself six feet tall and having a Baptist background. I do expect to see them both again, some day. Will he still be a foot taller than me?

I made that trip home on a few occasions when, for example, there was a three-day weekend, and a couple of buddies would come along with me. We basically went AWOL as we did not have passes to make the trip. We stuffed pillows under our blanket so when a casual bed check was made we looked to be in the bed. We would grab a train out of Syracuse and return at about two in the morning on the day we needed to be back in school. Fortunately, no one ever discovered the pillows under our blankets.

Blind Date

In one instance desperately needing a break in the action, I learned that the Blackwood Brothers and other southern style gospel quartets were scheduled for an All Night Hymn Sing, as they were called in those days, to be held in Detroit on the Saturday evening of my long anticipated three-day weekend.

I was able to contact one of my old Spring Arbor College buddies (who shall remain nameless because I can no longer remember who it might have been), and persuade him to meet me in Detroit for that event with a carload of Spring Arbor guys, and their dates. By this time, I had a car of my own. One additional requirement I laid upon him, was that his carload was to include a date for me, as well.

All went well on the Saturday of the event. I drove all day, from Syracuse to Detroit, and met my Spring Arbor friends at Cobo Hall, that evening. To be sure, I was a bit disappointed with the blind date presented me, and really did not behave as gentlemanly as I might have, throughout the evening. Once introduced, I promptly forgot her last name, but no matter, or so I supposed. I was again with my friends, and I loved that southern style gospel singing. It was a great evening, until about 2:00 AM, when the "All Night Sing" came to an end, Blackwoods and Statesmens sharing the stage for a final song, a male octet rendition that caused the pillars to vibrate and nearly brought the house down.

It was then that I learned, the home of my date was roughly halfway between Detroit and Spring Arbor, and her parents were expecting to host the entire party at their home, overnight. Oh, boy. Well, probably a good idea, since I was exhausted after a day of driving and a night of handclapping. I was so sleepy that I could hardly keep the car on the road until we reached her home.

We arrived, and I could not believe the anthropological dream that awaited, as we walked into the home of my date, a house having walls covered with carved wooden masks, spears standing in the corners, and seemingly no end to this display of wonders gathered from the aboriginal ends of the earth.

I stumbled into bed, and slept the sleep of the dead, but was the first of our party to tumble out, the next morning. I found "Mom" alone in the kitchen, working on our breakfast. I could not wait to interrogate her regarding these amazing items all around me, but got no further satisfaction than, "Oh these are just a few things we picked up in our travels."

I wandered around the house examining artifacts and pictures, and thinking back on my days even before Spring Arbor College, when I was so intrigued by missionary stories, especially by such books as "Words Wanted," and "2000 Tongues to Go." Those books had sparked a real interest in linguistics, and were in no small measure the reason behind my current enrollment in the Air Force Russian Language program.

I reflected on a trip I had made several months ago, returning from a Michigan vacation to my base in Texas, and engineering a side trip to Oklahoma University that I might spend 24 hours visiting the Summer Institute of Linguistics in session there. What an incredible experience it was to sit in those classes, observing those budding linguists interacting with Native Americans from various tribes of the west, learning to learn exotic languages, reducing strange sounds to phonetic symbols and again reproducing those sounds now recorded in their notebooks.

What an experience to listen to a presentation much anticipated by these student missionaries, a riveting lecture given by the highly respected linguist, Dr. Kenneth Pike, early member of Wycliffe Bible Translators and longtime president of the Summer Institute of Linguistics, as he reviewed a book called "Flatland." Flatland was a two dimensional world, in which lived a two dimensional individual who Dr. Pike referred to as "Flatlander." Dr Pike explained how Flatlander had somehow made contact with an inhabitant of a three dimensional world. He related Flatlander's exceedingly difficult attempt to comprehend this three dimensional person, this additional dimension, this new world, thereby illustrating to his audience of future translators the immensity of the problem one faces in crossing a cultural line, as is so critical in translating the Bible into the language of a new and exotic culture.

As I stood there looking at lances and arrows and photographs of native Ecuadorians, as all these memories were washing over me, at last, at last, the pieces snapped into place. "Words Wanted," authored by Eunice Pike, "Flatlander" the lecture of Dr. Kenneth Pike. I knew Dr. Pike was a professor of linguistics at the University of Michigan in Ann Arbor. We had just slept the night in Ann Arbor.

That is when I remembered the name of my blind date, niece of author Eunice Pike, daughter of linguist Dr. Kenneth Pike, Spring Arbor coed - Barbara - Pike.

Back to Texas

June rolled around and with it our graduation ceremony. This session at Syracuse had been a long and difficult chapter, one which I was thankful to have had, but one which I would not care to repeat. It was unquestionably the most challenging nine months of my life.

I drove to San Angelo in my well-used Chevrolet to continue my school. The car used a lot of oil and I had very limited confidence in it. There was opportunity to sell it to another fellow in my class who gave me three hundred dollars for it. I used that money to purchase an old Buick from yet another serviceman. It needed shocks and rode like a big old boat, but seemed quite reliable and I was happy. I heard a month later from the irate purchaser of the Chevy that it had dropped the transmission. I recalled how I had gasped in disbelief when he took the Chevy for a "test drive" and while moving forward, he slammed the car into reverse. He came back to report that the car had a sound transmission. I can imagine why he lost that sound transmission and I can't say I felt sorry for his bad luck. I'm just thankful it held together until I got his money.

Now that I had wheels and a heightened sense of independence, I attended a local Nazarene Church on weekends, as there was not a Free Methodist Church to be found in San Angelo. I made some young friends there and we occasionally double dated at a restaurant. I learned to eat "real" Mexican food during my time in the city. I would leave that restaurant, a fire breathin' dragon.

Once when I still had the Chevy with a Michigan license plate, I approached it in the parking lot and noticed that it was sitting next to another vehicle with a Michigan plate. The numbers on the two plates were in exact sequence, one number following the other. What are the odds of that, especially when a thousand miles from home? Turns out the other vehicle was owned by a young man with whom I had gone to school, and our plates had been purchased on the same day in the same office.

There is not a lot to be said about the schooling I received while at this base. It was again a very challenging time. Among the subjects studied were certain types of electronics, radios and antennas. There was significant polishing and expanding our skills with the language, skills such as learning to write a form of Russian shorthand and typing Russian text on a Cyrillic keyboard. That typing skill had to be attained after hours, the time taken from our free hours in the evening. Most of the students spent their evenings in the typing room for many weeks. Since I had taken typing in high school and spent long hours then to become quite proficient as a typist, I made the transfer to Cyrillic quickly and tested out within a week or so.

Once I finished school, I received orders to ship out to Japan for a two-year tour of duty. However, the departure date was some distance into the future, so I just hung around the base for a month or more, assigned to busy work such as "policing the area," which means picking up spent cigarettes. I drove the Buick to its new home to Michigan and left it there. I had accumulated a month of leave time which I spent at home before flying to San Francisco. From there I continued by air to Honolulu.

Hawaii is wonderful, I think. We sat down there to refuel, and we had two or three hours to kill. Of course, we were not permitted to leave the airport. But I hear that Hawaii is nice. Soon we continued on to Tokyo and Misawa Air Force Base, my new home a way up north on Honshu, the main island of Japan.

Land of the Rising Sun and the Falling Snow

Japan is an extremely interesting country made of three large islands and a seemingly infinite number of small ones. Tokyo, Kyoto, Osaka and most of the cities having names we are most familiar with, are on Honshu, the central and largest island. Kyushu is a large island to the south, as is Hokkaido to the north of Honshu. Still farther north is another sizable island, Sakhalin, which was once part of Japan until stolen by Russia nearly a century ago. Hence the Russian sounding name.

The three islands span an enormous distance from tropical areas on Kyushu to Hokkaido with long and frigid winters in the far north. From monkey hunting in the south (at least permissible 60 years ago), to bear hunting in the north. At the southern extreme, there is a hunting season for monkeys, or at least there was 60 years ago, and at the other extreme, there is a bear hunting season in the north.

Tokyo is pretty central to the main island and to Japan. Four hundred miles north of Tokyo is Aomori, Honshu's northernmost prefecture, (county), which contains a village aptly named Misawa, meaning "Three Swamps." It is here on the shores of Lake Ogawara that the large Misawa Air Base and the USAF 35th Fighter Wing is located. Approximately 3500 US personnel and another thousand local nationals are employed on this base. The main road into and across the base climbs uphill beyond the base for another couple of miles to a detachment, a small "sub-base" at which resides the 6989th unit of the USAF Security Service. This detachment was to be my home and place of work for the next two years, sharing barracks and workspace with other "voice intercept processing specialists" and with airmen commonly referred to as "didily-boppers," guys who were trained in the use of Morse Code.

Upon my arrival at the airbase I rejoined some of my friends from language school who had arrived ahead of me. They took me downtown on my first evening in Japan, to a little restaurant where for a few cents, (actually a hundred yen,) one could buy a huge bowl of "soba" noodles and of course the standard large bowl of rice. The rice in Japan is good, much better than I was used to in the states. However, I didn't think I could handle a large bowl of rice with nothing on it or mixed into it. So, the waitress broke an uncooked egg over the rice and that provided some lubrication. I soon was eating plain rice and enjoying it as much as did any native of Misawa.

The streets of the "machi," the town, were often muddy when it was rainy or when the snowfall, sometimes as much as two hundred inches annually of the white stuff, was receding. My first purchase with my yen, the currency of Japan, was a pair of "mach boots," G.I. lingo for rubber boots that pull over one's stockings and were the accepted footwear of Japanese National and G.I. alike, when walking along the muddy streets of the machi. A pair of mach boots would set you back only two or three dollars, and they made a lot of sense on the muddy streets of Misawa.

Speaking of G.I. lingo, there was much of that to be learned. At times when I first arrived, I could hardly understand my friends who spoke this new-to-me language that was a mix of spectacularly imaginative English and wounded Japanese.

On the other hand, it was interesting to listen to the Nationals speak their own form of English. I recall a time when I was taking my clothes to the laundry where Japanese ladies where sorting and washing the clothes. Suddenly one of them held up some socks, shouting, "How com-u, G. I. all time-u no change-ee sock-u? All time-u stink-o, stink-o."

As I traveled around the country from time to time, I ate often in restaurants, getting comfortable with sushi, the occasional tofu and rice, rice, rice, even having a passing acquaintance with such delicacies as squid tentacles, fish head soup and whale meat. Only once did I order "American food" in a Japanese restaurant. After that mistake I always went with the native cuisine.

I loved to get away from the base and off into the hinterland where G.I.'s were a novelty to the local populace. Often when riding a train moving at a snail's pace through a station, I would drop the window and for a hundred yen, purchase a sack lunch from a vendor running along the dock beside the train. The sack lunch was actually a little box made of balsa wood which contained some sushi or fish and rice with an assortment of pickled vegetables, and of course a pair of chopsticks. A fine lunch it was and filling. I found it humorous as I would slide the cover off the little box and begin eating lunch with the chopsticks, knowing that every eye in that passenger car was upon the G.I. with chop-sticks. At some point I would suddenly look up and chuckle as instantly every head would drop, every eye would be upon the floor.

I learned enough Japanese to get around, to read the schedules in the train station, and so on. But on occasion I would encounter a problem. Once I asked for a cup of coffee and a bowl of ice cream. That combination was apparently not commonly ordered in Japanese restaurants, and the waitresses supposed they were dealing with a miscommunication. I finally convinced them that yes, I really wanted an ice cream and coffee, but it was certainly more difficult than ordering a hamburger with catsup in Arkansas where the waitress responded with no more than "Kay-et-shup? You must be a Yea-an-kee."

Many were the adventures while riding the train in Japan. Many are the stories I might relate, but alas, one will have to do. Closing out a 3-day leave, I was returning to Misawa from Sendai, two hundred miles to the south, on the last connection available that evening. Exhausted, I dozed off in the waiting room and awoke to see my train pulling out of the station. I made a run for it. Clearly – and typically - it was filled to overflowing with humanity. I managed to catch the lower step of the last door of the last car as the train pulled away. That was as close to boarding the train as I could manage. People were hanging out the door and hanging onto the stair railing. I turned with my back to the train holding a stair rail with each hand, placed my suitcase on the second step and held it there with the back of my leg.

Away we went through the night as black as pitch, rolling along the ragged coastline, through numerous tunnels with the stone wall close to the end of my nose and when not blowing through tunnels, hop scotching across bridges over the Pacific where it cut into the mountain's edge, one could only guess how many hundred feet below. After lengthy periods of time the train would pull into a station but always it seemed, the platform was on the landward side of the train. It was still black as pitch on the ocean side and I had no idea what was below me.

After a number of such stops we did finally enter a station which had a lighted platform on my side. I was able to jump down and run up the rails to enter a much nicer car, the one for which I had actually purchased my ticket. I did note, however, that people were looking at me rather strangely as I entered. Only when I visited the restroom did I understand why I received those looks. In the mirror I saw a black man, black as the night I had been riding through. When that steam engine sailed through those tunnels, it covered everything in the tunnel with soot; even the G.I. on the last step of the train. But thankfully, I reached my destination on schedule and even if a bit groggy on the next morning, I was not found to be AWOL from work.

To whom should one show respect in Japan? It can be quite confusing to a foreigner. Only once, as I was riding the "densha," the electric train, did I stand up and try to give my seat to an old woman who had none. Every eye on that train, even the old woman's, was staring at me in disbelief. Embarrassed, I retook my seat, making a sad mental note to never again offer a seat to an old lady in Japan. A bit later, I saw that same train come to a complete stop at a crossing and wait for an old man to amble across the tracks. Slowly then, once the man had made his way across, the train started, tooted a goodbye and continued its run. One shows honor where – in the eyes of the culture – honor is due.

While riding my bicycle down a country road I once observed a farmer plowing his field with a team of horses hooked to a one-bottom plow. The farmer was walking before the team, holding the horses by the bridal, leading them across the field. His wife was walking behind and holding the plow in the ground. On that day, clearly this farmer did not think a wife's place was in the kitchen.

I and the people I worked with every day had all been awarded a Top-Secret security clearance before we could begin the job, or in fact before we could finish our schooling. They were exciting days, those cold war years, as my tour included the days of the Cuban Missile Crisis and the first manned flights into space.

We were a pretty close-knit bunch of fellows, although we represented a variety of interests in our off-duty activities. There were the motorcycle guys who bought small Hondas and loved to ride them around the countryside. There were the photography buffs taking advantage of the inexpensive cameras and equipment available in Japan and the many interesting things to be photographed.

I was able to purchase a small automobile which I rarely drove far from base because the roads were often so impossible, the gas so expensive and the car so underpowered. It was an imported vehicle, a BMW Isetta, which is difficult to describe because it was so strange. There was one seat which would hold two people, maybe three very small people. The only door was not on a side but was the entire front of the car. As the door opened, the steering wheel folded out of the way. The steering wheel was on the left side, although in Japan the right side was the right side. The handle for the manual gear shift came out of the left wall of the car, and the pattern was reversed from the normal gear shift pattern. It had a three hundred cubic centimeter engine, a motorcycle engine which was just behind the seat and accessible from the rear. The car had virtually nothing by way of springs, the seats were not much better, and the rear wheels were within a few inches of each other, giving the impression that the car was a tricycle.

I once took Ralph for a ride, the gentle giant who during school had visited my home at Christmas time. It was a very snowy winter as they all are in northern Japan, and any snowplow to visit our detachment was quite a novelty. We were driving on a road having deep ruts frozen in the snow. The car slipped sidewise so that the rear wheels were one rut too far to the left, and we were going nowhere. Ralph unfolded himself and got out of the car, walked around behind, picked up the rear bumper and sat the car back into the proper rut. He returned to his seat, folded himself in again, and we continued down the road.

I kept my Isetta until time to return home and then sold it for the same price I paid for it. It had not been very practical but it had been a lot of fun.

We linguists and diddly-boppers worked inside a compound, an area surrounded by a high chain-link fence containing a few buildings. Windows were high in the walls and when open to allow some breeze during the summer months, loudspeakers sat in the open window blasting music to anyone outside the compound. Of course, we had to flash our badge as we entered the compound gate for work each day. Just outside the gate was a little booth where one could buy a coffee to help keep him awake during the long "mid" shift, midnight to eight in the morning. The coffee was made and sold by Japanese Nationals who apparently thought the standard G.I. came with a cast iron gut, as the solution they sold us required a tablespoon of sugar before we could choke it down. But at five in the morning, desperate for sleep, we would go back for a second or third cup.

Earthquakes in Japan are quite common and pretty much taken in stride. I sat in the library one day and watched the book cases tipping back and forth, the hanging lights swinging as though in a breeze. I waited a bit and sure enough everything returned to normal. No books tumbled from the shelves.

86

 One morning I came off the night shift, had my breakfast in the mess hall, went to my barrack and climbed into bed. I had barely gone to sleep when I awoke again to find my bed walking across the floor. Jumping out of bed, I ran down the hallway to stand on the porch at the end of the barrack. The other barracks, long skinny buildings, appeared to be writhing like snakes and the telephone poles looked like long fingers waving, "Naughty, naughty". Remarkably, nothing came apart.

There was a period of six weeks or so when I was for all practical purposes, confined to quarters, being sensitive to my appearance during a time of some rather extensive dental work. But over time the monotony became unbearable and required something new and different. One thing new and different was the little theatre in my area, new and different due to my background and resulting inhibitions that precluded prior attendance at a theatre.

One day I decided to attend that little theatre, my first visit ever, to such a house of immorality. Nervously, I approached the building watching to see that no one might be looking, watching the heavens for any telltale flash of lightening. Thankfully I got inside without experiencing any heavenly intervention, got a box of popcorn and seated myself in the shadows.

I had no idea what was playing but that was irrelevant at the moment. Only later did I realize what a rare stroke of good fortune that my first flick was a movie to be long remembered, a movie destined to become one of the all-time great classics, Audrey Hepburn's "Breakfast at Tiffany's." I recall Christmas in Japan, a rather lonely occasion, for which I took my old, old Free Methodist hymnal with the dark blue (or was it black) hardcover, bundled up against the cold of December in Northern Honshu and wandered over to the chapel. The door was always unlocked, and I went in, sat down at the Hammond organ and wiled away the afternoon playing and singing those old hymns. It got me through.

Sundays came and went. At times my work schedule reduced me to one option, attendance at the little chapel on the hill, to hear the message brought by the chaplain and occasionally provide a solo for others in attendance. Other times I was able to don my mach boots and walk through town to a little Japanese church I had discovered. Many of the same hymns were sung that I had heard, growing up. Words were written in hiragana, (a phonetic syllabary of about sixty characters) which I could read quite well, so I was able to sing along with the little congregation. I also learned to recognize books of the Bible when they were called out, and of course I knew my numbers, so was able to turn to passages as scripture references were announced. I cannot say that I got much from the message beyond that, but at least people knew where I stood and with a few of them I became very good friends.

Traveling Japan

When I had opportunity to get farther away from the base on a weekend, I would take the train south, halfway to Tokyo, to the city of Sendai which was home to the northernmost "Jiyu Meso-disuto Kyokai," the Free Methodist Church. Somehow, I had gotten the address of the church, but finding it in this huge city was quite another story. I stopped someone on the street and explained to him in my crippled Japanese where I was going. He gave me a rather lengthy series of directions which apparently, I must have understood because I came directly to the church. I think regarding my comprehension of Japanese, that event may have been my finest hour.

On such trips to Sendai I would spend a day or so in the home of the pastor, and attend church there. We became good friends, and I was treated to various adventures such as an "ofuro," a bath in a wooden tub of water with a fire burning in the fireplace beneath. The Pacific near Sendai was quite a tourist attraction as near the shore were a gazillion picturesque little islands with stunted trees clinging desperately to their craggy shorelines. Of course, we visited that attraction. Sadly, not many years ago a tremendous tsunami rolled over the area, causing many deaths and great destruction not only to the little islands but to much of the city.

Another highlight of my adventures in Japan was spending two weeks of accrued leave time visiting Osaka, a large city in central Japan with much history behind it. The Sniders, Laverne, Lois and 5-year-old daughter, Carol, were Free Methodist missionaries from Canada assigned at that time to Osaka Christian College, our denomination's school which over the years turned out thousands of school teachers. I spent a brief period of time visiting in their home, doing some sight-seeing, and enjoying a surprise visit with my former Spring Arbor pastor, Vernon Dunckel, who was visiting Japan at that time. I recall an evening spent singing hymns together with the family, Lois at the piano. Lois had not been in good health of late, had just experienced the loss of a parent in Canada and had been unable to return home at that time. It was gratifying to hear from Laverne the next morning, "Last night was so good for Lois. She slept throughout the night for the first time in many months."

The first week I traveled with the Sniders to Shikoku, another smallish island just off the southern coast of Japan, to take part in a week-long event for teenage Free Methodists, an event which in the States we would call a youth camp. It was held in a hotel just across the sidewalk from the Pacific Ocean. In the morning there was a variety of classes attended by the young people; following that a break for lunch and in the afternoon free time which for most meant swimming in the Pacific. In the early evening we had the final meal of the day, sitting on the tatami mats in a large room with our legs crossed beneath the long tables where we were served real Japanese cuisine, the fishhead soup, the sushi, the tofu, the rice, rice, rice. Choir practice followed and then a message by one of the youth pastors to close out the evening. The highwater mark of the week for me was the evening service in which I joined three of the native pastors in a male quartet to provide some gospel music, a four-part A Capella rendition of a hymn which we sang, of course, in Japanese.

At week's end we returned to Osaka to wash our clothes and on the next day continued driving east to a resort area in the mountains northwest of Tokyo. Many missionaries in need of some R & R were vacationing there, not only people from the US and Canada, but from Brazil, Europe, the Philippines, Taiwan, Korea. It was an amazing week. Every day we visited little vendors' shops where we selected fresh vegetables and fish to bring home for the meals of the day. Every evening we attended a service in a large wooden tabernacle reminiscent of ones I knew in the States. There was a bookstore in the rear, open during the day and after services. There was a volunteer choir which practiced a new song every day to be presented during the evening service.

What held the greatest interest for me during that week was the sight of the many young children of all those missionaries, playing together on the playground or in the sand box, children of various shades and colors, children who spoke a variety of native tongues from around the world, but who still got along famously in their play because of having a common language in Japanese which they all spoke not as a second language but as another native tongue.

Nakamura-San

It was perhaps ten miles or so from my station in Misawa to the next city, quite a sizable one in fact, Towada Shi which was the center of government for the Aomori prefecture. A densha, an electric train, made several daily runs between the two cities. My first solo adventure away from the base was to ride the densha to Towada Shi. However, I misjudged the return schedule and missed the last return trip for the day. I was stuck. Some adolescents were nearby, talking and having a good time. They spotted me and saw opportunity to practice their English. As we talked in their broken English and my very limited Japanese, they came to understand my dilemma. A couple of them ran to the home of their English teacher, Mr. Nakamura, for help. They brought Nakamura-san back and introduced us. Nakamura-san could speak English marginally better than his students, and so we quickly got acquainted. He suggested that I should spend the night at his place. Fortunately, the next day was not a work day so it was a workable plan and we followed through accordingly.

That was the beginning of our friendship, and for the rest of my stint in Japan I often spent time with Nakamura-san in Towada Shi. He taught at a large school having students of seventh and eighth grade ages, which we would call Jr. High. To give some idea of its size, there were nine teachers on staff whose sole responsibility was teaching English. Mr. Nakamura's desk was in one of the teachers' rooms; a huge room it was, having fifty or sixty teachers' desks in rows up and down its length.

My rotating "trick" schedule at work meant I often had free time during the day, so I was frequently able to take the densha to Towada Shi for the day. When the electric train rolled into the city, I would go directly to the school, walking into the teacher's room where Nakamura and his friends would welcome me with a hot green tea, the Japanese beverage of choice. When the students arrived, I accompanied Nakamura-san to class and spent the day in front of his room, modeling the English lesson for the students, helping with their pronunciation and so forth. Over time I became friends with a number of the teachers as well as many students who looked for any opportunity to interact with me.

On several occasions I spent the night at Nakamura's place. The house was of wood construction, a rather flimsy wood at that, so it seemed, with window panes in the sliding doors made of some sort of oiled paper that held up to the elements pretty well. The floors were covered with tatami mats, woven straw which made a soft comfortable surface to walk or sit upon. Anyone entering the house left his footwear at the door, as using shoes on the tatami mat was never done. In the center of certain rooms was a fire pit, a hole in the floor holding a big iron pot called a hibachi, in which a wood fire was kept going during the cold winter months. A shortlegged table stood over the hibachi and then a fabric, a sort of cross between a table cloth and a quilt, was spread over everything. The table was large enough that at least four people could sit around it on the tatami mats, legs crossed beneath the quilt so that everyone at the table was kept toasty warm. It was a simple matter to keep the upper part of the body warm. One just wore enough clothes.

I slept in Nakamura's home in the dead of winter when the temperature in the house was in the zero degree range. My bed was a thin mattress rolled up and put away during the day, but rolled out on the tatami mat at night. A thick quilt was spread over the mattress and another one, perhaps four inches thick spread over that. Between the quilts was a large stone heated in a hibachi and rolled into a blanket. This was placed near the foot of the bed and certainly felt wonderful on chilly feet. I had no problem staying warm and in fact woke up bathed in sweat.

Another teacher, a friend of Nakamura's, once took us to the home of his father who was a rich farmer by the standards of Towada Shi. That was clearly the case because he had a walkbehind garden tractor to till the rice paddies and fields of his farm. It was also obvious because his farm was on a hillside. This was a distinct advantage especially when there was a stream or other source of water uphill from one's farm. The farmer could then contour his rice paddies like stair steps and from the water source allow water to flood first the top paddy, then the next one down,

94

and so forth. The farmer who didn't have that advantage had a rough time keeping the paddies flooded, and perhaps a rough time eating during the next winter. I saw such paddies with the mud dried up and cracked, rice lying dead in the paddy. It was not a pretty picture.

I was given some tall mach boots to wear, and we all went into the paddies to plant rice. It certainly raised my regard for those farmers who spent all day stooping over to plant rows of little rice plants in the mud.

On one occasion the teachers even took me fishing. As I recall we didn't have very good luck. But, no matter what; we had a great time.

The first day of the new year is a big deal in Japan, with fireworks and parades and ceremonies at which one pays one's respects to the deities, whether Shinto or Buddhist. But I was invited to Nakamura's place to take part in those New Year's festivities. Of course, there were fireworks on the eve, trips to the various shrines, and then the overnight as just described, sleeping on the tatami mat in the frigid house. On the next day I was the guest of honor for some entertainment, song and dance, music from a three-stringed samisen, all provided by geisha dancers in beautiful kimono. These were not professional geishas, mind you, but girls from Nakamura's English class who dressed up to play the part for my enjoyment. There were lengthy parades to be observed, with many floats sporting ferocious dragons and all kinds of fearsome creations made of colored tissue paper and flowers.

For my part, I invited Nakamura-san just before Christmas to the chapel on the main base where many G.I.'s and their family members presented Handel's Messiah. I even had a solo in that production.

Graduation day from the Towada Shi School occurred in late March. Of course, it was a big deal for the graduating students. The ones with the best grades went on to the next level of school. For the less fortunate their school careers were now concluded. They would need to pick up some skill which would become their livelihood.

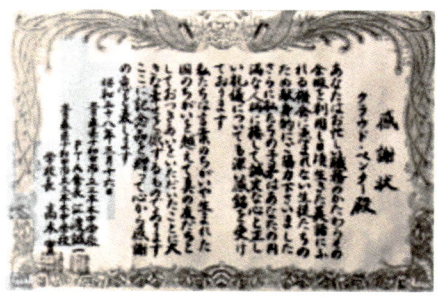

Not only was the school administration on the stage but dignitaries from the city and the prefecture were present for the occasion. At one point in the ceremony I was invited up onto the platform to be introduced and explained to the parents in the audience. I was presented with a very formal looking scroll (and a translation in English) thanking me for my assistance with the English students. The principal and the mayor of Towada Shi came forward to bow and shake my hand, and all in all they made a pretty big deal of it. I even have a school yearbook with my picture in it.

So, I did my part to cultivate good relations between the US military and our host country. I doubt that my superiors ever heard about it, but I don't mind. I had a wonderful time.

Donning my Civvies

But the day came when I had to make that decision: Would I sign up for another four years or pack it in and return to civilianhood again. I loved Japan, I loved my job in fact, and I had become very good at it. But I could not bring myself to commit to another four years. Instead, I finished out my tour of duty and returned home in the Spring of '64. It had been a difficult, a positive, a wonderfully rewarding four years of service for my country and nearly 60 years later I still feel very good about having had a part in that.

The USAF gave me my last free flight, back to San Francisco in the spring of '64. My parents and sister drove to California to meet me, and we vacationed on the way back to Michigan, visiting several of our national parks on the way.

It was good to be home. There were adjustments to be made; Dad occasionally shouted at me when I drove his pickup truck on the left side of the road. It was time to begin looking for work and thinking about returning to school in the fall, but I confess, I dragged my feet just a little bit. I needed a breather.

Our church in Durand had a new pastor, recently immigrated from New York State, a bit east of Syracuse. He invited me to join him for a quick trip which he needed to make back to his home. I went for the ride and to keep him awake. He dropped me at Syracuse to visit friends while he completed his business. On our return trip I again bailed out at Roberts Wesleyan College, our Free Methodist college near Rochester, leaving the pastor to stay awake on his own. He was upset.

Within a day or two, I stumbled into a job in Rochester, and called home with the news that I would not be returning. My parents were sorely disappointed, but I explained that I had a job and come fall, would be starting school. In the end, I wound up returning to the New York State University system, but still hung around the periphery at Roberts, supposing it might be a good place to find a wife. That turned out to be the case, although she remained elusive for another couple of years. In the meantime, I worked two jobs and then leaving one job in the fall, returned full time to school. Interestingly, in spite of the busy schedule I managed to earn better grades than I once did at Spring Arbor, and even found myself on the Dean's list. It makes a difference to have a vision. Mine at that time was to teach English.

My sister, Lois, was working in Durand and driving a brand new Chevy Malibu for which Dad had cosigned. When she saw how I had walked into a good paying job at Kodak, she decided she would like to try the same thing. She dropped her job in Durand, nearly causing Dad to drop his teeth. But within a week of her arrival in Rochester she was also employed by Kodak and continued to be so employed for many years.

In the summer of 64, Lois and I began attending the Parma Center Free Methodist Church located about ten miles north of Rob-erts Wesleyan College. The Parma Center Church was one of the first churches in the denomination, a building which by now was more than a hundred years old and in rather tough shape. It was pas-tored by Layman Fletcher who lived in the nearby parsonage.

Over the next several years I purchased a series of European-built automobiles. The first adventure was an Italian Fiat, a rather well used puddle-jumper with poorly padded seats, a leaking radiator and an inclination to overheat at the most inopportune time. I soon wearied of carrying along the gallon jugs of water and anti-freeze, and moved on to something a bit more reliable.

Since I was now working and stockpiling a few bucks, I was able to purchase a new vehicle, this one being a lovely red French-built "R8" Renault with the trunk under the "boot" and the motor over the rear axle. My R8 seemed to be a favorite target, however, and after a year or two, all four sides had sizable deformities, most of them the result of others at fault.

In time, I upgraded to a wannabe luxury-vehicle, a British-built Triumph 3000 which was imported very briefly. It was a classy white four-door sedan with deep blue carpeting on not only the floor but also the walls, and a pretend wood dashboard and console.

At about the same time, my sister, Lois, acquired another Triumph, a "Spitfire" roadster with removable canvas top and seating for two, seating so low that one's posterior barely cleared the pavement below. it was a blast to drive, so when Lois saw the need for a more practical vehicle, I was happy to take the Spitfire off her hands.

One might ask if this preoccupation with foreign vehicles became an expense. I will admit it is a good question and leave it at that. However, I will relate one or two adventures with these several immigrants.

Came deer season in New York State and I drove my wonderful red Renault, still intact and unspoiled, north into the mountains (so-called,) of northern New York, rented a little motel room, and prepared to take the woods on the opening morning of the season. Of course, a hunter, ideally should be in the woods when the sun comes up. I drove down a wandering snow-covered track that split the dark pines until I reached a little stream spanned by a rustic bridge. Well, actually it was spanned by a couple of logs which once supported some planks, long-since decomposed. The logs were in pretty good shape, however, flat on top, and they appeared to be about the same distance apart as were my little French tires. I approached the stream, got out to check things and discovered that sure enough, it was a perfect fit.

Driving onto the logs, I opened the door, hung my head down to check that all was well beneath the car, and so crossed the stream and continued on down the trail, laughing as I imagined the thoughts of any hunter who might happen across those tire tracks in the snow.

I took a vacation from work in the summer of '66. I was twenty-five, free as a bird, enjoying a footloose vacation in my little Triumph Spitfire. The Spitfire was a nifty little sports car with a top of black fabric and two seats which sat very low to the ground. It had a very short manual shift stick coming up from the floor. The Triumph was an absolute blast to drive. It was the perfect vehicle for traveling the Appalachian roads.

Triumph Spitfire, a British two-seat
sports car introduced in 1962

Navigating the steep hills and sharp curves of the mountains, wandering over the torturous back roads of Kentucky, I made an impulsive decision to attend the Sunday morning service about to begin in a tiny one room church nestled among the hills.

There were perhaps twenty people in attendance, singing lustily, following the words which the pastor lined out to them from the only hymn book in the building. I suppose it was quite a novelty for this little church to have a visitor, particularly a young man of my age. I would guess that the pastor knew exactly what he was doing when he called on Sister Ruth, a young lady among the regular attenders, for an impromptu testimony. Sister Ruth seemed a bit reluctant at first, but at the pastor's urging she responded enthusiastically and at considerable length.

Came time for the offering, and the pastor made an impassioned plea for a little extra to apply to their outstanding mortgage, a figure that had been hanging over their heads for some time. The figure, it turned out, was twenty dollars.

In those days I didn't have a charge card to my name nor a lot of

101

cash on hand either, so it was a concern that I not run out of twenties before returning home. Even so, I deposited one of them into the basket as it came by, never dreaming that the offering would be counted while we sang the next song, and the amount immediately reported back to the little congregation.

Following the song, the usher informed the pastor from the back of the room, "Twenty-one dollars and thirty-seven cents."

The pastor responded, "Praise the Lord. One dollar and thirty-seven cents."

The usher raised his voice to say, "Pastor, that was TWENTY-one dollars and thirty-seven cents."

The pastor seemed confused for a moment. Then he began to really praise the Lord. "First thing in the morning, I'll be going to the bank to clear off that mortgage!"

Following the message, a happy congregation greeted the obvious source of the unexpected contribution, and the pastor invited me to his place for lunch. We talked at length over a can of spam until I said my goodbye and crawled into my little roadster.

As I disappeared over the hill and around the next curve I could still see in my rearview, a happy penniless pastor standing by the road and waving at my cloud of dust.

What Happened at Parma

When I first attended the church at Parma Center I met and was befriended by a trio of siblings, Doug, Don and Darlene Reiman, all students at Roberts Wesleyan. They knew me from my days of singing in the Spring Arbor quartet although I did not know them at that time.

Pastor Fletcher had retired from pastoring at least once, but was still a full-time employee at Kodak. He recently had taken on the additional responsibility of pastoring this ancient church at Parma Center which was about to be closed due to a dwindling congregation. He was determined to build up the church again. It so happened that the Painters and Reimans came along at just the right time to assist him in his vision.

Darlene Reiman also assisted me in a manner that I had not anticipated, as she brought a guest, yet another Roberts Wesleyan student, to church one Sunday in '66 and introduced us. Esther Holiday and I quickly became more than just friends, which certainly had been Darlene's intention when she made the introduction.

Esther was the eldest of five children, and had been away from her family for several years as she was attending school. Her younger siblings still lived with their parents and her Grandma Slaughter, in Fruitland, Idaho, near the border with Oregon. Esther was a lonely biology major at Roberts.

During that summer of '66, Esther was working on campus to

make a few dollars. I was working midnight to eight at Kodak while taking 12 hours per semester and six per summer session at Brockport College, part of the New York State University. For our first official date, we went to see the Hill Cumorah Pageant, an enormous extravagant annual outdoor spectacle presented on the hillsides near Palmyra, New York. It was a depiction by enthusiastic "brothers" and "sisters," members of the Church of Latter Day Saints – a depiction of the early history of the Mormon Church, or at least the good parts of its early history. One might argue, not such a romantic beginning, this first date, but a spectacular spectacle it was, and a fun first time together.

Esther's father was a scholarly book-loving Free Methodist pastor who was then filling a hard-scrabble circuit in eastern Idaho, and working as a common farm laborer to support his family. Besides the family of five kids, a grandmother lived with them, occasionally even two grandmothers – and a cat named Joe Cool. It was not until months later when I visited her home that I could really appreciate their modest quarters and the sacrificial lifestyle required of Esther's family due to her father's call to the ministry. It was then that I saw throughout the house the furniture that her father had built, dressers, tables, the boys' homemade bunks with rope netting supporting their mattresses. But that visit was almost a year away.

I asked Esther for a second date, this proposal a bit more audacious even, than the first, but she agreed. We drove to Michigan, eight hours each way, for the weekend. Both of us being of Free Methodist lineage, it seemed appropriate to me that Esther should visit my family as they were camping at the annual camp meeting of the East Michigan Conference. This yearly event was a time when perhaps 2500 people from 100 churches came together for two weeks, and it had been an important highlight in my summers as I was growing up. Many were the friends and relatives who were there on that weekend; it was the perfect time to introduce them to Esther, and she to them.

It soon became clear to me that Esther was the right one; and fortunately, she quickly came to hold a reciprocal opinion. By Christmas we were engaged, the phone call was made to Idaho to request and obtain the official buy-in from Esther's papa, and the deal was clinched with — not the standard engagement ring, mind you, but a new Singer sewing machine for Esther.

That departure from the conventional continued to produce returns for nearly fifty years before the machine finally died, and was perhaps the wisest acquisition I ever made, second only to the bride, herself.

The school year wore on, a bit slowly it seemed to me; more trips to Michigan at Thanksgiving and again at Christmas. With a wedding coming up, I again dropped out of school for the spring semester, and picked up a second full time job, working 80 hours a week, often more, until Esther's graduation.

Heading to a Wedding

In the spring of '67, Esther graduated from Roberts Wesleyan with a major in biology. Her mother came from Idaho to see Esther walk the stage and claim her sheepskin, and to find out who was this guy to whom her daughter had become so attached. Following graduation, the three of us drove to Idaho in my brand new blue Chevy, towing and living in a newly purchased 13 foot Amish-built hardtop camping trailer. The ladies slept in the trailer at night, while I had my own private quarters in the car. We took time to visit a few national sites on the trip west, Craters of the Moon and Mt. Rushmore among them, but the main focus was on reaching the final destination.

We eventually reached Fruitland, Payette County, Idaho, and following a frantic week of preparations were married there in the little Free Methodist Church, on Sunday afternoon, June 18, 1967. It was a wedding on a shoestring, and a thin shoestring at that, but one that was long remembered by the local citizenry in attendance. There were lots of flowers which came not from a florist shop, but from the local gardens of friends. There was lots of music for the wedding, which came entirely from the wedding party.

My family drove from Michigan for the wedding, of course. My sister, Lois, was one of the bridesmaids, as were Mary, Esther's sister, and Shanna who would soon become Jim's bride. Esther's brother, Jim, was best man. Her brothers, David and Sam were the ushers. The ushers seated mothers and guests until taking their places next to Jim's station. Jim, however, moved from his place to the minister's place behind the alter, as the ceremony began. Preparing for the ministry, Jim got his first experience officiating, until the bride's father delivered the bride to the alter. At that point, Jim reassumed his place as best man, and Rev. Dad Holiday took over to finish officiating the wedding.

Regarding the music, Jim, brother of the bride, sang a solo at one point in the ceremony, as did Lois, sister of the groom. The groom sang "The Lord's Prayer," and the bride joined him to sing "Savior Like a Shepherd Lead Us." For that duet, the bride's mother left her seat of honor to accompany on the organ.

The high point of the reception was a beautiful wedding cake made by one of the local women. Wedding and reception, both were a resounding success, the bride was beautiful, the dress was gorgeous, the guests were happy and the gifts were numerous.

We enjoyed a few days of anonymity in Boise, honeymoon hotspot and tumbleweed capital of Idaho. Details which can be shared: I got a speck of something in my eye which required a visit to a doctor. The offensive particle was removed and I wore an eyepatch around Boise. We enjoyed a day at the well-known Boise Zoo, well known locally, not so much on a national level, but no matter. We still share fond memories of the friendly elk following us along the fence, eventually draining my entire bottle of Dr. Pepper, as it was poked through the wire.

We returned to the Holiday home in Fruitland to load the wedding presents into the little Amish house trailer, to say our thankyous and goodbyes and to begin the long trek back to New York. Driving north through Montana and Glacier National Park, we passed by snow banks still melting along the roadside in late June, and crossed into Canada. Route 1, the major route spanning Canada, stretched on endlessly, so it seemed, with but one event memorable enough to be remembered.

It was late at night, a dark, moonless night with Esther at the wheel, pulling the trailer between walls of tall pine trees and around a sharp curve where suddenly a bear appeared in the headlights. The car was moving at a very good speed and there was no way one could have stopped in time. Somehow Esther managed to whip the speeding car and its trailing payload, around that big black blob without touching him, and the newlyweds continued on their way. Surely there were angels surrounding us that night.

We crossed out of Canada into Michigan's Upper Peninsula where the locals are known as Yoopers. Traveling the long bridge spanning the Straits of Mackinac, we continued south to my parents' home. It was a happy arrival, a very happy arrival in fact, since the gas tank was nearly empty and the billfold entirely so. In those days one didn't carry a pocket full of plastic, at least this one didn't. Dad loaned us a few dollars to complete the trip home, and without further adventure we crossed Ontario, arriving at our new home not far from Parma Center, just in time to return to work the next Monday.

Beginning Together

We moved into our new upstairs apartment in the village of Hilton, sleeping on a mattress on the floor for a few days until we procured a bed. I brought cushions from the Amish trailer into the apartment and placed them on a couch frame constructed of 2x4s.

But we soon visited a nearby furniture store and purchased a beautiful bedroom suite, a couch with a fold-out bed and a dinette set with six chairs. We took out our first loan from the bank to pay for these items, and paid it off over the next year or two. The dinette set served us for thirty-five years or more, by which time the chairs were getting rather worn. The heavy flex steel couch was incredible as we had it for more than forty years and it was still like new when we sold it, the fabric still showing almost no sign of wear. We still have the bedroom set, now fifty years old, and except for a couple of dings from moving experiences it looks like new.

Having now settled into our new apartment, the first matter on Esther's agenda was landing a job. She did that soon, and became a 3rd grade teacher in the fall, at the school in the little village of Kendall, where she taught for three years as I was finishing my college and beginning my own teaching career. I began as a 5th grade teacher in the same little rural school district, in fact the same building where Esther taught. Our teaching careers overlapped for about a year and a half before Esther dropped out to attend to raising a family.

Once we began teaching in Kendall, it made sense to live there, also. We moved to the area, living in two or three rented locations until we were finally able to purchase a small four room house having a sum total of 720 square feet and a walk-out basement. That became our home for the next twelve years or so.

Esther and I paid a visit to a friend from her childhood years who lived some distance south of us in New York State. It was a sleepy afternoon; the ladies were making conversation in the living room while I was lying on the couch and studiously observing the inside of my eyelids. Suddenly two words from their conversation broke through the fog and I sat straight up to ask, "What is a knitting machine?"

 A knitting machine turned out to be an incredible device having a bed of 200 parallel needles, actually latch tools, upon which one might create a universe of beautiful knitted items. This required further investigation and the first thing to be learned was that the cost was out of sight. Even so, we soon found a shop in Buffalo where knitting machines were sold, and went to investigate. Wow, the bright colors of the cone yarn, the textured designs of the garments, all those mechanical components working together flawlessly, each zip of the carriage across those needles resulting in another perfect row of knitting. The possibilities of this machine caused the imagination to soar into the stratosphere. There had to be a way. Turns out, there was.

If one became a dealer, one could buy machines at a considerably reduced cost. The "Lickety-Split Knit Shop" was born. Of course, "customers" required an inventory of cone yarn; soft, bright, beautiful imported stuff it was, wool and acrylic, alpaca, angora, so many colors. We began creating sweaters for the kids with pictures of deer or toy trains, lacy floor-length dresses for Donita, three-piece outfits for Esther.

Being an elementary school teacher, I took a couple of machines to my classroom in December and taught the kids how to knit and stuff Christmas presents for their parents; Christmas tree hangings, Santa Clauses and so forth.

In time I could take an order for a garment, measure the customer, lay out a pattern, calculate increases, and crank out the requested item. As skills developed and techniques improved, with the advertising in place and the business cards distributed, sales were realized which then required knitting lessons for new customers and the acquisition of more inventory, more machines, more yarn.

There was the time when school shut down early because a major snow storm was brewing. By the time I got home there was already a deep drift blown across the driveway. I drove into it as hard as I could. I opened the hood and threw a blanket over the motor. Coming into the house I pulled a big sheet of plywood over the doorway before shutting the door. That was it. For a week we were in the house. Roads were impassable for days. I loved it. I sat at that knitting machine for hours and days, just cranking out clothes for the kids. Now, that's my kind of a blizzard.

It was such fun for a decade until other activities slowly squeezed it out of our lives. But thirty years later we still have our demonstrator machines on the shelf and incredible amounts of that beautiful yarn. So, if you know of a potential yarn customer, please point that one to me.

In the summer of '69 I was invited to join a quartet of singers representing the Rochester chapter of Youth for Christ. They were losing their bass and I was highly blest to become his replacement. Great musicians they were, and David Anderson, our pianist and the arranger of most our music was beyond incredible.

Nearly every Sunday night the Christianaires, as we were then called, later the Joy Singers, presented a concert in a Rochester area church, and were followed with a message by Fred Thomas who was the director of the local chapter of YFC. For a time, our concerts were augmented by one or two  numbers on a wonderful trio of trumpets played by gifted students from the Eastman School of Music. We had a weekly radio program, visiting the station periodically to record three programs at one time which were aired over the next three weeks.

In time we added more voices to the group, bringing our number up to six, then eight, and for a time twelve singers in the group. The Joy Singers were well known across the area and kept very busy not only with the concerts but in recording a half dozen long-play albums. At the same time the YFC chapter was expanding significantly, at one point having nine fulltime staff members leading a great many YFC clubs in Rochester schools and making a remarkable impact on the Rochester community. I was very blessed to be a part of that program for a ten-year period spanning the decade of the '70s.

A Decade to Remember

For Esther and me, the decade of the '70s was also remarkable for another reason and at times quite difficult as we were beginning our family. In 1970 our first child was born: Marcus, who, we soon learned, had apparently suffered brain injury from a difficult birth. He never reached the milestones that parents watch for in their children: standing, walking, feeding himself, potty training.

Two years later, Donita was born, and after another year, Soren, our second son. Can you believe, Soren was the same story as his older brother. Both sons lived on a liquid diet delivered through a stomach tube. Both suffered seizures, not infrequently, both endured repeated pneumonia. Wherever we went we always carried their suitcase filled not only with diapers but a variety of medications, large syringes for feeding them, small syringes for injecting them. Difficult days for sure, but made tolerable by friends from the Parma church who learned to care for the boys and gave us a break now and then; by members of the Joy Singers who blessed us with their companionship.

Soren lived about two and a half years, finally made perfect just as we were coming into the Christmas season, In 1975. Donita was three years old at the time of his passing. She tells of waking up in the night. to see a bright figure enter the room, pick Soren up from his bed and carry him out of the room.

Her memory is vivid to this day. She believed then and does now that the figure was an angel and insists that she was not dreaming. She awoke the next morning to learn that Soren had died in his bed during the night. I don't believe she was dreaming, either.

One year later, again just entering the Christmas season, Marcus joined his brother. Both of them had notable home-going services as a quartet from the Joy Singers was a part of those services and sang many songs, childrens' songs such as "Children of the Heavenly Father Safely to His Bosom Gather," and "Everything's All Right in my Father's House where there's Joy, Joy, Joy."

We were now a family of three and so thankful for Donita, our little princess. One day in March or April when the snow was beginning to abate and patches of grass here and there were peeping through the snow drifts that Donita looked out the front window and exclaimed, "Oh, look! A summer spot!" Little did she know that right then she was the summer spot in our lives.

Building a Church

Early in the '70s a property ideally located for a new church building became available for purchase. It was a large corner lot a mile north of the old Parma Center Church and just south of the village of Hilton. There was a house located on it, but not in very good condition. We purchased the property, repaired the house and rented it out to generate some income while we continued with our plans.

A building fund was established and in two or three years we had sufficient funds or pledges lined up so that with the sale of the old building (which became a tire repair shop) we were able to put up a beautiful new building and later a new parsonage on that corner.

Esther and I continued on at Parma Free Methodist for a few more years. I was the building fund treasurer during the building period, and later the church treasurer when the two funds were merged. Of course, we got stuck at one time or another, with most every job invented by the Free Methodist Book of Discipline: Sunday School superintendent, trustee, you name it. It was a busy period in our lives, but rewarding.

On one occasion we invited an elementary student from my class to go to church with us. She told other students about that and some of them wanted to come also. Soon we were driving our nine-passenger station wagon loaded with a dozen kids or more, to church every Sunday. It was not long before we asked a friend with a car to help pick up these kids. Then two friends with cars, and then another one. In not too much time we needed a school bus –

and got one which the pastor drove, to pick up dozens of kids every week and return them home.

It was really an operation as our rural school district was quite expansive. I would ride the bus with the pastor as it made a loop through the district, while Esther in the station-wagon made several loopty-loops to pick up several kids each time and rendezvous with us to transfer the kids to the bus. For a period of time, perhaps a couple of years, we brought several dozen kids to church, until they got older and became discouraged by the lengthy time spent on the bus. Only eternity will tell what was the end result of that operation.

Pretend Farmers

In 1978, Eric was born, and in 1980 Deanne, the last one to join our family. Both were planned caesarians, and we now were blessed to have three healthy kids. Almost too healthy, sometimes. I would have to remind myself every time Eric put the soccer ball through a window, "Hey, do you want a kid who can kick a soccer ball?"

It occurred to me one day, that we could avoid the cost of buying milk for the family if we had a couple of milking goats. We had enough land and it seemed like a great idea to me. Esther didn't agree. In a sud-

Nubian Dairy Goat

den flash of inspiration, I took the family to visit the Rochester Zoo, specifically the petting zoo with the baby goats. Soon we got a couple

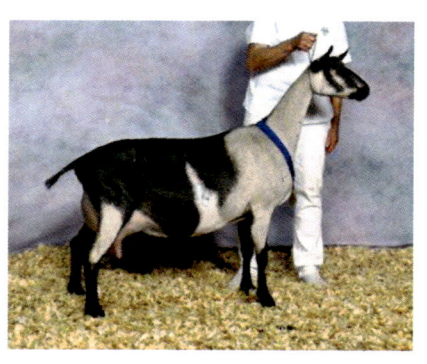

Alpine Dairy Goat

of Nubians, those goats with the long floppy hanging ears, such as are often present in travel flicks filmed in Africa. Then we got more goats, registered goats, none of your scrufty mongrels. Purebred Alpines they were, with good milk production in their lineage.

We also needed a good buck or two. Why would we need a buck, you ask? For the city folks, goats do not give milk until they give birth. For that to happen you need a buck around.

As the number of our milkers increased, often as many as twenty of them, we built a specialized milkhouse for the animals. A ramp led up to an elevated runway about a foot wide that traveled around the perimeter of the milkhouse and led to a descending ramp at the other end. The runway, elevated at thirty inches or so, made a very convenient height to milk the goats standing on it. Along the runway were four stations, each having a little sliding door in the sidewall which could be opened for access to a box behind the wall holding an allotment of grain to be eaten by a milker while she was being milked.

In groups of four, we would release the milkers from their pens; they would go charging madly into the milkhouse, up the ramp and around the runway, each stopping at her station to eat her grain. We would snap each goat collar to a short chain at each grain box, and then we could milk them at our leisure. When all four were milked, we would unsnap their chains and they would go plunging down the ramp and back to their pens.

There were several dairy goat raisers in our area, each specializing in his own breed of goats, Alpine, Saanen, Nubian, and so forth. Since we were all breeding for increased production, we needed a good way to track the production of each animal. We were aware of Cornell University's official testing program for milk production which was used by large dairy farms, cattle dairies of course, to keep an official running tally of annual pounds of milk production per animal, and analyzed a monthly milk sample for butterfat, protein and numerous other factors. It seemed like just what we needed for our herds, but it was much too expensive.

The solution, we found, was to attend Cornell's training program and become state licensed testers, ourselves. We did exactly that and then were able to conduct monthly surprise visits to each other at milking time, weigh the milk from each milker and collect a milk sample which went to Cornell for their analysis and the monthly report generated for each milker. Now we knew for sure, which animals should be part of our breeding program and which we should not include. We learned how to give the goats their annual shots, do minor surgery (sutures and all), find and pull reluctant kids when the birthing was difficult. At times, our herd numbered 50 animals, with 20 milking does. At times, we'd turn five gallons of milk per day into cheese. We made butter and ice cream. Lots of ice cream. With our Nubians producing six or seven percent butterfat in their milk, man, that was good ice cream.

We learned to buy a couple of week-old calves early each spring. All summer and fall, we would pour the excess goat milk down those calves, and when they reached maybe 800 pounds, hang them up in the back yard, and then put them in our big chest freezer. Wonderful eating all winter. In that manner we raised our family on goat milk, baby beef, goat meat, lamb, (we expanded), and the produce from a huge garden.

There was a day in the dead of winter when the well pump died. There was no water available for the animals. That was a serious problem. The only solution that evening was to carry water from the creek.

The creek bank was steep and deep in snow. I chopped a hole through the ice large enough to fill the buckets and made a number of trips carrying a five-gallon bucketful in each hand up the bank and some distance to the barn. It is surprising how much water a pair of 800-pound calves and forty goats and sheep can drink. But I finished the chores and all was well. I thought.

The next morning, I arose at the usual 5:00 AM to do the chores, and as I was dressing, I suddenly experienced a pain in my side as though kicked in the slats by a horse. Esther got up and did the chores while I sat gasping on the couch. When she came in from the barn, I was beginning to feel a little better. Not much, mind you, but I was not about to make out lesson plans on short notice for a substitute.

I went off to teach school that day and the next... Little by little I felt better, although as we were getting along toward spring, I was becoming shorter of breath. Soon I could not walk across the room without stopping to "blow," to borrow an expression from Tom Sawyer and Huck Finn.

I went to see the doctor. A couple of X-rays later, he told me, "I don't know why you don't have pneumonia. You've been walking around all winter with a collapsed lung." He wanted me to go directly to the hospital. I explained that I had to get in a load of hay and grain for the critters before any operation. I did that and then turned myself in to get my lung "blown up" again.

A couple of weeks later I sang a solo at church. When one is as loud as I was in those days, it takes a lot of lung power to sing a song. I returned to my seat and felt the old lung going again. Fortunately, it was not painful this time, merely a strange sensation in my side. With only a week or so of tests before summer vacation, I finished out the school year and then told Esther I had to get my lung fixed again.

The third time it happened the doctor sent me to a Rochester hospital where they did a more extensive surgery which now prevents any more of these spontaneous (as they called them) events. Following my recovery from that I was finally back to normal and could do anything I wished except going deep-sea diving. All in all, it made for an interesting spring and summer.

We got colored sheep for hand spinning fleeces, a spinning wheel and carder, and learned how to spin wool. To this day, Donita has a cedar chest full of unspun angora from her own "herd" of angora rabbits. Perhaps someday she will get around to spinning that angora wool.

My favorite among the sheep was a wonderful big silver colored Lincoln ram who cost me big bucks to purchase and many miles of driving to bring to his new home. Being a ram and a Lincoln, the only fitting name for him was Abe Ram Lincoln. Abe was a real gentleman and covered with beautiful ringlets of

Lincoln Sheep

122

silky wool growing a foot of length in a year. Sadly, one night, Abe got out of his pen and found the supply of grain where he gorged himself, the kiss of death for a beautiful Lincoln ram. We found him lying lethargically in his pen the next morning and could not bring him back around. Poor Abe, gone but not forgotten.

Another great guy was our pure black ram, a Finnish Landrace for whom we drove across several states and brought him home in the back of our multipurpose station wagon. We decided that he also deserved a memorable name; his became Huckleberry Finn. The Finnsheep is a breed noted for its multiple births, twins and triplets being the norm with occasionally four or even more in a liter. So, to introduce Finnish blood into one's flock means Finn-cross ewes will be more prolific and thus more profitable.

Huck was a man after my own heart; not a big guy but notable for his determination. On one occasion, unable to gain access to the next pen wherein resided a young lass for whom he had eyes, Huck battered a pair of holes through the outside wall of the barn; the first to make his exit and the other strategically located for reentry into the neighboring pen.

Our barn was some distance from the house, so in the cold nights of early spring, (the wee hours seeming to be the lambing time of choice,) we would have the intercom turned on between barn and bedroom. We could then hear a ewe in the throes of labor, don our winter attire and head for the barn.

A need for help at lambing time was not unusual; assistance in turning a lamb around or pulling a reluctant baby. Sometimes it was not even my own ewe in distress. I recall receiving a call for help from a friend, then crawling out of my warm and cozy bed in the frigid pit of the night to dress and drive half an hour for sake of someone's ewe that could not eject her wooly young.

Sometimes when I think back, I wish I had all the money I sank into those animals, but we ate well, and the lessons of responsibility that the kids learned, was worth it all. In any case, that part of our lives began slowly to change as a result of a circumstance in the early '80s.

I had been teaching fourth grade, and then second grade, for a dozen years, and frankly, I was getting a bit weary. One day the principal said, "Claude, you need to pick up some evening classes, get a little computer literacy." Computers were coming onto the scene and I always wondered how one could make letters appear on a monitor by typing on a keyboard. It didn't make sense to me. I told the principal, "Sure, why not." After about three evenings of classes, I'm telling myself, "Hey, this is fun. Why should I still be teaching school?"

Career Change

I returned to the college where I had earned my teacher certification, for an interview with the head of the math/computer science department, I explained to her that I wished to add on another major in computer science. She asked about my college experience to date, I explained the majors in English, education and foreign language. She asked about the math background. Rather skimpy it was. She shook her head. "I don't think we can help you. You need pre-calc at a minimum to enter the computer science program. And besides, the classes are always filled up by our regular full-time students." I told her, "Thanks." But I told myself, "I'll show you, Lady."

The next session was to begin in a month or so. I signed up for pre-calc, got a college algebra book and worked my way through it. I took the class in pre-calc and earned a B. Now I was on my way. Three part-time years and forty credit hours of math and computer science later, I bailed out of teaching. To be honest, I didn't have the new job lined up, yet, and but for the grace of God and assistance of a lot of friends, would have lost the house by the time I got to working the new career. But I think if I had never taken rash action, I would never have taken action of any kind. I did finally get that first job as a programmer in late '87, and at the time of my retirement twenty-plus years later, I was still looking forward to going to work every day. They called me names like "systems engineer," "software designer," database administrator," and so on. I worked the entire time as a contractor or a consultant for a consulting agency. Except for a year early on, when I was placed at Kodak, my entire history as a developer was at Xerox, working on one project after another.

Of course, the work days were longer than when I taught school, and I didn't have the lengthy summer vacations. I drove a considerable distance to work; obviously this kind of work is typically found in larger population centers, not the kind of place where you can raise goats and sheep, cats and kids. I drove about 50 or 55 miles, a bit over an hour each way, to work. But I wouldn't have traded it off to return to those school teaching days, not for anything in the world.

A few years into the new career, I bumped into the "chairperson" of the math/computer science department with whom I had not spoken since that interview, and described to her how things were going. I didn't tell her I was earning three times what I had last earned as a teacher. She shook her head and simply said, "I never thought you could do it." I could have answered, "I know. That's why I did it."

A New Church

The years of our marriage can be divided into five stages based upon the places where we worshipped, with those stages being roughly 10, 5, 10, 20 years in duration and finally 10 and counting. I have referred to events of our lives during the first 10 years at the Parma (NY) FM Church, to the birth of our three oldest and the passing of two of them, to being part of the building program of the Parma Church, singing with the Youth for Christ group, and so on.

Although we are anything but church hoppers, a situation arose at Parma which at length became intolerable, so we moved our family to the Brockport FM Church, a fairly large and growing community of Believers. We attended there for five years, and frankly, did little more than act like sponges during that time. We felt so exhausted from the previous 10 years - actually it had been 13 for me - that except for some singing and song leading, we just spent the time relaxing and getting it together, again. It was a good time. The two youngest were born during this period, Donita was elementary school age and those years in the Brockport kids' program were important in her life.

We should have seen the next 10-year period coming, but it caught us off guard. We had some good friends at the Brockport church, a young couple about our own age, who entered the ministry during that time, and were assigned to a new church plant, the new Hamlin Free Methodist Church, located not far from where we lived. Initially their weekly service was on Sunday afternoon, so on the second week of their services, I said to Esther, "Ahhh, why don't we pay them a visit at their new church, just for kicks. We'll have time to get there following our service at Brockport." Was that a bad mistake! I wound up leading the singing, that Sunday - and the next - and well, you have the picture. For a couple of years, we kept a foot in both camps, as we felt the kids needed the more mature program of the established church, but in time we moved our membership and our commitment to the new church plant.

Again, we were in the thick of it, eventually church treasurer again, wouldn't you know, eventually another building program, and so on. This time it was much tougher, since we never seemed to be able to grow a good core of people who were truly committed for the long haul, and because of a series of rather bad mistakes which the conference made along the way. In time, our Genesee Conference became rather proficient at the whole church planting thing. Unfortunately, they gained a wealth of good experience at our expense. For several years we maintained attendance numbers of 50 people, or maybe 60, but little by little, things began to taper off, getting so bad that I finally handed the song leader's responsibility to the pastor, and I became the piano player. Now, I hope you can appreciate how desperate we had become!

A New Home

We had lived for too many years in our little four-room house, and needed badly to find a place that was a better fit. I explained to our realtor that we wished something in one of only two school districts, rather small rural ones, because they were the only schools I wished my children to attend. Quite soon he found a place for us in the Lyndonville school district, a ten acre mostly wooded piece of land with an old farm house built about 1905 which had been unoccupied for a couple of years. The price was right, in fact, the price was a steal. But someone else put in a better offer than ours and so we lost our opportunity. Nonetheless, we continued our preparations, getting the current place ready for selling. A couple of months later we got an unexpected call from the realtor who said the house was back on the market. Apparently, the prospective buyers were not able to get financing. We jumped this time, and our offer was accepted.

The new back yard

Our current place sold quickly and for an unexpectedly high price, and we had no trouble getting the financing and making the move.

We moved the family, the sheep, the goats, the barn, yes the barn, and we were in business.

Eric was in second grade and Deanne just entering kindergarten, so it was a good time for them to make the move. Both did well in the Lyndonville School District and developed friendships with some wonderful people with whom they are good friends yet today.

Donita was just entering her four years of high school. She did well in her new school, although she never was able to develop the close friendships that she had in her previous school. I remember a conversation I had with her math teacher during those years. He said, "Donita is a very special young lady. I don't understand why she doesn't have a circle of friends around her. They are the losers." She developed a real interest in writing, which we were happy to see happening, and we encouraged her as much as possible. She was always a part of the yearbook staff, and became the editor during her final year of high school. At her graduation the yearbook adviser presented her with a box of red roses. Her mother sprouted one of the flowers and planted it, so that Donita's rose grew in our flowerbed for years.

But we now lived at the very edge of the district. Our house was the last stop on the school bus run. That meant that with every dousing of lake-effect snowfall, sometimes a foot overnight, I was in the driveway at four or five in the morning, clearing enough snow from our downward-sloping driveway that the bus might back in and turn around without getting stuck. That was a lot of snow.

As the kids grew, they turned into musicians. Donita had several years of piano in her elementary and junior high school days, and later in college, a minor in voice. Eric and Deanne both took violin lessons for a number of years, with Eric later switching to the viola. Both took piano for several years, as well, and were part of the school band, Eric with the trombone and Deanne with the French Horn. She also played the marimba for a time. The crazy kid would come home from school with a different instrument every little while, and seemed able to play anything she wanted to. I remember how impressed I was as a student at Spring Arbor College, with the "perfect pitch" ability of a friend there, never dreaming then, that someday my own daughter would have that same remarkable gift.

I soaked a lot of money into lessons and instruments for these kids over the years, figuring it was an investment in the Lord's work. I thought, if someday, my three kids were doing their part to enhance the music programs of their respective churches, the investment would surely be worthwhile. Time has proven it to be so. An unexpected bonus is that I often sing back-up behind them when they serve as leaders in their congregation.

There was an event which we attended as a family, just as Donita was entering college and the other two were about Jr. High age. Although my memory is fuzzy regarding some detail, I do remember what was most important, and it must be told. I remember that there was a door prize to be awarded at the end of the evening, a Macintosh computer. It was not much of a computer by today's standards but in the eyes of the kids, it made for a pretty impressive door prize.

Time came to pull tickets out of the hat and as that was happening, I suddenly had a feeling that Deanne was going to win that Macintosh. The ticket was pulled and I was not surprised as the name of the winner was read: "Deanne Painter!" Naturally there was lots of excitement and spirits were high as Deanne received her door prize and we carried it to the car.

As we were driving home, I began to sense that Deanne was sobbing softly in the seat behind me. Of course, I asked her what was the problem. Her response, "Donita needs that computer at school. I told God tonight that if He would let me win that computer, I would give it to Donita to take to school." What can a parent say to that?

Donita headed off for Spring Arbor University, and began pursuing her interests in writing, music and acting. She volunteered for the yearbook staff, and became very involved in production of the college yearbook. There was a strange development when she was less than half way through that first year. The editor decided he was in too deep, and he abandoned his responsibility. Donita was offered that office as a freshman and brought the job to a successful completion.

She then worked for a time, pulling more money together, until returning to Spring Arbor again. During her time off, she acquired some great work experience, first clerical type stuff at Kodak in Rochester, then writing for a couple of different newspapers and magazines in the Jackson, Michigan area. Once she returned to

Spring Arbor, she became editor of the campus newspaper for most of the rest of her tenure there. She crammed her four years into eight, the last half year being spent in a program for journalism students in Washington DC.

When at length she graduated, she had a lot of good experience behind her, and had no trouble finding her first position with a newspaper not too far from Spring Arbor. She continued to live in S.A. for a couple of years, as she worked that first job. However, wanting to "go where the action is," as she put it, she eventually landed a job as a reporter for a newspaper in Rockville, Maryland, just north of DC. She was there for a year doing a job that was very stressful but from which she gained a world of experience which has since served her well. But that comes later in the story. Meanwhile...

A New Synagogue

Along about 1990, or so, (we had now been struggling for eight years at the Hamlin church plant), Esther's mother began telling her about some interesting TV programs she was watching, and materials she had subscribed to, which talked a lot about end time prophecy, and such stuff, things that Free Methodists really never get into very much, and it was all sort of going off the deep end, it seemed to me. And a large part of that talk seemed to be about Jewish people who were coming to the Lord, and how there was a new something developing which was called the Messianic Jewish Movement with Messianic Jewish congregations in the larger population centers. There was a lot of talk about Christians who needed to learn more about their Jewish roots, and yada, yada, yada. All very interesting, I suppose, if you happen to be interested, but I was a third generation Free Methodist, fifty years in the denomination, married to a FM pk (preachers kid), both of us graduated from Free Methodist schools, and if I cut myself, I bled Free Methodist blood.

But along the way, something went wrong. Esther began reading a few books recommended by her mother, and watching some of these Jews on TV, and at length, persuaded me to do the same. And I began to remember how my mother, in the late forties when I was just a kid, talked to me about something she found incredible, that after 2000 years, Israel had become a nation. In one day, it happened, just like the Old Testament prophecy said. And the barren desert was beginning to grow fruits and vegetables, just like the

Old Testament said would happen. And the language, virtually dead for nearly two millennia, was being spoken again, just as the prophecy said. It didn't mean anything to me then, but now it was coming back to me, in the context of the things I was hearing from Esther and her mother.

One day, Esther said, "I wonder if there is one of these 'Jewish churches' in Rochester?" She researched the question, and found that, yes, there was a place named "Congregation Shema Yisrael." And they met on Saturday morning. More time elapsed, and eventually, early one Spring, she talked me into taking her and the kids to visit this place on a Saturday morning.

 We found a four-story masonry building that didn't look at all like a place of worship. We walked into the door, wondering what we were getting into, and were greeted by a rather slight lady with very dark hair and an attractive smile, who said, "Shabbat shalom, my name is Kim. Is this your first time at Shema?"

She handed us a packet of information and a card to fill out, and helped us find a seat in a rather crowded sanctuary. Many of the men were wearing a kippa, the little skull cap, and the tallit, or prayer shawl. We were not prepared for what was to come. This was to be culture shock, big time.

As the service opened, everyone began singing a song in Hebrew. Then they began quoting Scripture in Hebrew. "Shema Yisrael, Adonai Eloheinu, Adonai echad." Fortunately, they followed in English. "Hear, O Israel, the Lord thy God, the Lord is one." Then the worship team took the floor. For the next forty minutes, everyone was standing, singing, sometimes in Hebrew, sometimes in English. Besides the singers and piano player, there was a sax player, a guitar player, and can you imagine, a big fat guy beating the daylights out of a set of drums. And worst of all, over in one front corner, there was a circle of people dancing to the music. A far, far stretch from the Free Methodist Church I knew.

The music was very different, usually in a minor key, usually with a real beat to it. I had never experienced people worshipping like this before. The leader was not an instructor, but simply a pattern to be followed. He didn't tell the congregation, "Now turn to page 397," "Lets sing this like we mean it," "Lets repeat the chorus without the piano." Nothing was horizontal, everything was focused upward. He just sang to the Lord, songs not "about" the Lord, but addressed "to" the Lord. Everyone joined with him, and the music just flowed from song to song without interruption for forty minutes. And that dancing was so incredible. It was beautiful. Those people were worshipping with their hands and feet and their whole body. I wept my way through most of that first praise and worship session.

Following the announcements and offering, the rabbi in tallit and kippa spoke for at least 45 minutes. It went like a flash. I had never heard teaching like this before. It was not only powerful; it was as though he held the Old Testament in one hand and the New Testament in the other. And there was a constant cross referencing between the two. "See how this was foreshadowed in the Old Testament. See how this was brought to completion in the New Testament." And the rabbi used different words. He never said, "Jesus" or "Christ." He spoke of "Yeshua," or "ha Mashiach." And Yeshua died on a tree, not on a cross. Later, I would learn the very valid reason for the different terminology. I would learn that "Yeshua" is a form of the Hebrew word, "salvation." Then it made sense that the angel instructed Joseph, "You shall call His name, Yeshua, for He shall save His people from their sins."

Following the service, we visited "The Fig Tree," a bookstore in the building, which was filled with all kinds of books written by Messianic Believers in Yeshua, or about subjects pertaining to Messianic Judaism; lots of tapes and CD's of that wonderful music recorded by Messianic musicians, and all kinds of "Judaica" - tallits, menorahs, special dishes for Passover celebrations, Hebrew language learning materials, and so forth. It was wonderful. How shocked I would have been that morning if someone had told me that Esther would be the manager of that book store for nearly 20 years.

It was a few weeks before we elected to try Shema Yisrael again. After all, it was a drive of fifty miles from home. On the other hand, I drove it to work every day. So we went. And the next week, and the next.

Now, Eric and Deanne, in their early teens, were not at all excited about this turn of events. They already went to church on Sunday. And to get rolled out of bed at 6:30 on their only day off, that was a real downer. Moreover, they didn't buy into this Jewish stuff, at all. (Donita, of course, was off at Spring Arbor College, and didn't have to deal with it.) But Mom and Dad prevailed, the kids raised Cain and then came along, and we began "double dipping" as they call it around here, when you attend two congregations.

At the same time, the Hamlin church plant was entering its darkest hours. In spite of everything, attendance had fallen to perhaps twenty people and the conference was covering our mortgage on the new building to prevent losing it. Our "core" now consisted pretty much of only our family and the family of my younger sister, Carolyn. Her husband, Al, plus Esther and I were the only three to meet with the conference superintendent for that final meeting when we voted to turn out the lights. The building was sold to the Wesleyans who still continue there, many years later, with an attendance no better than we commonly had.

So here we were now, without our church. It seemed to us that Yeshua was calling us to stand with His blood brothers. Clearly, He is doing great things with the Jewish people, today. For 1700 years, most of the Church has repeated that God is finished with the Jewish people. But we had seen otherwise. How wrong the "church" has been.

I understand that this must all seem so distant to most Christians, particularly those who do not live in the large population centers where a concentration of Jews is more likely. But that makes it no less valid or factual. We were thankful to be living near a location with a fair-sized Jewish community, roughly 25,000 in Rochester.

We have come to understand not only that we are very near the end, but that Jewish people are going to play a major, major role in the fulfilling of the prophecy associated with End Time events. Why else has "ha Satan" engineered such incredible persecution of the Jews over the centuries? If God cannot bring His plan to fruition, then Satan wins. Yeshua, himself, said that He would not return, until His blood brothers and sisters say, "Blessed is He who comes in the name of the Lord." So "ha Satan" did everything possible to prevent the first coming of Yeshua. Since that didn't work, he is now doing everything possible to prevent the second coming of Yeshua. For him, that means simply, to remove the Jewish people as a factor.

But God has made it clear in His word and through His prophets that He will never allow this to happen. That is why there has always been a remnant of His Chosen that survives every holocaust brought against them. We believe prophecy is unfolding around us. And we have decided that we will not be content just to sit on the sidelines watching it unfold, but we want to be a part of it, right in the middle of it. And we are having a ball. I sometimes tell people that I've been in congregations before where I've worked this hard, but never where I've had this much fun.

As I said earlier, Eric and Deanne were not at all taken with the idea of losing their Saturday, it being a hundred-mile round trip and a two-hour service, especially since we continued faithfully in the Free Methodist Church for the first three years that we attended Shema Yisrael. Once we had closed the doors of the church at Hamlin, we began attending Edgewood Avenue, another large and vibrant Free Methodist Church in Rochester. That meant another 100 miles of travel every Sunday. But we were merciless parents, so Eric and Deanne attended with us right through high school.

It must be mentioned that the rabbi we heard on our first visit to Shema was a man named Jonathan Bernis, the man who had founded Congregation Shema Yisrael and one of the key figures in the Movement today. The message we heard on that day was his final regular message to Shema, as he was about to leave for the CIS, the former Soviet Union. The Iron Curtain had just been rent in twain and Rabbi Bernis was about to begin a work in the Jewish

Rabbi Jonathan Bernis

population centers of those countries. His replacement at Shema Yisrael was a new rabbi on the scene, a gifted man named David Levine. Thus, for my family, our first two years in the Movement were under his ministry. Rabbi David with his wife, Sandy, hails from Roanoke, Virginia. When he discovered Shema Yisrael, he discovered and quickly joined the Messianic Movement. Soon he became Shema's next congregational leader.

As we began attending Shema Yisrael regularly, we spent quite a bit of time in that wonderful book store, the Fig Tree. So many good books; so much to learn. Esther began to hang with the

Rabbi David and Rebbetzin Sandy Levine

bookstore manager and learn a few things about the operation of the store. At one point I said to her, "What would you do if you were given the opportunity to manage that store?"

Her response: "I'd grab it in a minute!" Little did we know....

It was about two weeks later that the book store manager quite suddenly left the congregation, and Rabbi David asked Esther if she would care to take on The Fig Tree. She took it on for the next seventeen years. Both she and The Fig Tree flourished during those years even like the tree planted by the rivers of water.

We were still attending the Edgewood Church with the hope of doing some bridge building between our congregations. The situation was this: Edgewood was a congregation of business people, educators, and professionals, and this church was in the very heart of the Jewish section of the city, only a few blocks up the street from the Jewish Community Center. I used to sit in that church and fantasize an impossible dream, "Wow, wouldn't it be wonderful if Shema Yisrael had such a property in such a location as this. Like people in most any church, no one knew what to do about all those Jewish souls; perhaps most never even thought about it. I think the high point of our adventure at Edgewood was a request that I lead a 13-week session of adult Sunday School classes named something such as "The Jewish Roots of Our Faith."

I went to Rabbi David for some direction, and we pulled together plans for classes on thirteen various related subjects which were to be taught by a number of people from Shema including Rabbi David, Rebbetzin Sandy, Jim Appel who is currently the rabbi there, and a number of others from the congregation. To say the classes were well received is a serious case of understatement. The sessions were the all-time best attended series of adult classes Edgewood had ever seen, with as many as 70 or 75 present for many sessions. I'm sure there was a lot of learning going on, but once the session was over, we saw nothing different; things appeared to be as they were before. Quite discouraging. But there is more to the story. It took two decades to be written and is still being written today. In the fullness of time I will tell "The Rest of the Story."

After two years at Shema, Rabbi David and Sandy moved to Eastern Europe, the Former Soviet Union, to assist in Rabbi Jonathan's developing work there, and Congregation Shema Yisrael was left in the hands of its third rabbi, Jim Appel.

The Kids' Stories

Over the next several summers, all three of my offspring were in Eastern Europe for one or several of Rabbi Jonathan's outreach events there. Eric was there for most of four consecutive summers, following which he brought a young lady back from St. Petersburg. They were married in September of 1999, in a beautiful outdoor wedding on a lovely warm autumn day. Rabbi Jonathan Bernis found an excuse to fly back to the States so that he might officiate at the wedding. Anya had been a regular in the St Petersburg congregation, Jonathan's first congregation in Russia. Anya's mama also flew in for the wedding and that required a Russian translator. So it can be said that it was a beautiful outdoor trilingual wedding. As things were winding down and Anya was getting into the car, about to ride away on the honeymoon, she asked, "Can we do this again?"

Meanwhile, Donita continued for a year or so, on her new job reporting for a paper in Gaithersburg, Maryland, just over the line from DC. She spent a very demanding year on that staff before being called by the editor of the "Messianic Times," a quarterly magazine which served as the voice of the Messianic Movement. Donita was asked to join its reporters' staff. She agreed and within a month was living in Jerusalem, the Old City, which became her home for two years.

Shortly after her arrival there, the senior editor left his position, and Donita was appointed to his position. (Shades of that yearbook, back in Spring Arbor.) Again, she found the work to be extremely demanding as she did not have adequate staff for support. There were times when she would call us in the middle of the Jerusalem night to request, "I must meet this next deadline, but I can't go any longer without some sleep. My alarm clock would never wake me up again. Please call me back in an hour."

After two years, the Jerusalem office was closed as a cost cutting measure and Donita worked the next two years in the home office located at St. Catherines, a bit east of Niagara Falls. She lived at our place in New York State, crossing the border daily as she made the hour-long drive to work. After two more years of burnout, she resigned from the Times to take a bit of a Sabbatical.

Following a break of a few weeks, Donita came on staff as assistant to the rabbi, Jim Appel, at our Congregation Shema Yisrael in Rochester, and was very busy there for the next seven years. She received a local ordination with the title of Administrative Pastor, as well as the title I've assigned her, Shema Yisrael's answer to the Swiss Army Knife because - she did it all.

Then Deanne, our little renegade, graduated from High School and began college at Roberts Wesleyan, the school from which her mother had graduated. Eventually she bailed out of the Messianic Movement, to our great disappointment, and began attending a charismatic church not far from Roberts. At Roberts she met a fine young man, very sharp guy with a wonderful tenor voice, one of those Mennonite types from northern New York State. However, this guy didn't quite fit the mold, which made him a perfect match for Deanne who stepped to her own set of drummers.

Deanne left Roberts after a couple of years to attend another local school, one at which she became a superb hair stylist and colorist. Brian graduated, and they were married and, bought a house in Rochester. Brian taught music in a city school, while Deanne, following a stint as a colorist in another person's hair salon, set up her own stylist's chair and worked at home. They continued as praise and worship leaders and in other capacities at the charismatic church I mentioned. In 2004, their first son arrived.

Meanwhile Eric took his child-bride to Michigan for a few months while he finished college and graduated from Spring Arbor University. During that time Anya also took some ESL (English as a Second Language) courses. They moved back to our home briefly but soon moved on to Jacksonville, Florida, because Anya wished to attend a school of Davidic dance and ballet, run by Believers there. Anya attended for several years, fulfilling an early dream of hers. Once in Jacksonville, they began attending Beth Jacob Messianic Congregation where Eric soon came on staff as the congregational administrator, and took up leadership of the praise and worship team, as well.

As it happened, some difficult days were soon ahead for the congregation, as the rabbi departed quite suddenly. The congregation was left with local speakers and various fill-ins for a couple of years. The first Shabbat after the rabbi's departure, Jonathan Bernis of Rochester/St. Petersburg "fame" came to speak to the congregation. He met with Eric who was now about 24 years old, and told him, "Eric, there are three key personalities who hold a congregation together. One is obviously the main speaker; one is the worship leader and one is the person in the office. The first one is gone and you are the other two." So Eric with much help from others, of course, did his part to hold things together for roughly two years, trial by fire, until a new rabbi was located who would move to Jacksonville and lead the congregation.

And who was that new rabbi? Eric's former rabbi in Rochester, David Levine, who couldn't coax Eric to join him in Russia was now returning with Sandy to the US, specifically to Jacksonville.

Truly the Lord must have a great sense of humor.

Russian Outreach

While this was all going on, Shema under the leadership of Jim Appel, began a food pantry ministry in Rochester, having in mind the many elderly Russian-speaking Jewish immigrants in the city, some of whom were Holocaust survivors. It was quite an effort with 35 to 40 volunteers involved in some manner each week. Every Tuesday food was brought in from a number of sources, but chiefly from grocery stores with outdated food that was still quite usable.

In the evening, volunteers with cars or vans would pick up many of those elderly people, particularly the Russian-speaking people and bring them in to Shema where they would fill their bags with food, take them to the cars and get a ride home again.

It was not long before some of the Russian speakers began asking questions. Who is this Yeshua we keep hearing about? We never learned anything about God. Could you teach us about Him? So by popular demand you might say, we began picking them up 30 minutes sooner and giving them a 30-minute service before they went for food. They would hear a song or two and a message by the rabbi which was translated into Russian.

I was one of the drivers and for ten years of Tuesdays, rain or shine, snow or ice, we rarely missed. In large part, for this reason, the family vehicle became a Chevy Astro-van, an 8 passenger with extended wheelbase and 4-wheel drive; a shelf built in the rear to offer more room for the boxes and bags of food. I usually had sev-

Love that Astro!

en passengers in the van, among them a medical doctor, two Red Army Colonels, an English to Russian translator of professional documents, an artist, and so on, skilled and educated people who over the years became my very good friends. I fully expect to meet some of them again on the other side.

Deanne, Brian, and their son Alex visited Eric and Anya at their new home in Jacksonville, developing some warm friendships with a number of people in the Jacksonville congregation. Now along came David and Sandy Levine and in 2005 Brian and Deanne couldn't stand it any longer. They suddenly announced: "We're going down to help Eric." Within four weeks, they had put their house on the market and sold it. Deanne went web surfing and found a great job opportunity for Brian to teach music in Jacksonville. She made the phone call; the school flew him down and hired him on the spot. Eric reserved an apartment that opened up next door to his own; everything happened, bang, bang, bang, and they were gone. Within two or three weeks of their arrival in Jacksonville, Brendan was born.

Now, unbelievably, my youngest is again a Messianic. And for Brian, it is quite a transition from Mennonite to Messianic. Now, as part of the congregation newly renamed Beth Israel, they soon

149

joined Eric and Anya as praise and worship leaders. For several years, they also conducted a large summer "camp" (a "glorified" DVBS for some of my readers) which attracted many outside families to Beth Israel.

Brian was a great hit at his new job, teaching for years at a Presbyterian day school in Jacksonville. Deanne gave piano and violin lessons for a time, until Audrey, number three, came along in 2007.

Anya came up to speed with her English in no time, got her citizenship in five years flat, and proudly voted for president in 2004. She became a manager for a Jacksonville bank, worked there for a number of years and in time had oversight of two, occasionally three branchs.

Remodeling the House

From about 2001 Esther and I were pretty much living alone in our big farmhouse between Rochester and Niagara Falls. Donita was with us for two or three years following her return from Jerusalem, but then moved into an apartment in Rochester. I continued driving 50 miles to work in Rochester every week day and to Shema Israel every weekend.

Our farmhouse in western New York was situated on a well-traveled two-lane highway which was parallel to and just south of the shore of Lake Ontario. It was a ten-acre parcel having only a 300-foot frontage but which reached a third of a mile back into the woods. Great deer hunting country, but I was always so busy working that I rarely got back into it. I had a rather large diesel powered farm tractor which I purchased soon after moving to this location and with its assistance, over time I cleaned out many large trees near the house, and managed slowly to push the frontier farther back from the road. This of course, meant more lawn to mow, so that I eventually got a John Deere riding mower and spent six to eight hours a week keeping the grass in check.

During this time Esther and I took on a new project, not realizing then how extensive the project was to become. When we had purchased our big old farmhouse of 2400 square feet built in 1905, it was for the most part in pretty good shape but terribly outdated. For example, it still had the original lath and plaster walls; some of it had been painted, some of it papered over, some of it still had its original face showing. The house was not well insulated, so keeping it warm in winter with the ancient gas furnace in the basement was not cheap. But we bought the place with the thought that in time we would remodel and bring it up to date.

We found however, that raising three kids who between them played most every musical instrument known to man, even tak-ing lessons on a few of them, was an expense leaving no room for re-modeling an old farm-house. Only after the kids were grown and gone, were we able to give the house some at-tention. And we could afford to do that only if we did the work our-

Esther stained and varnished ten new six-panel doors and the stairs

selves - work at which for the most part, I had virtually no experi-ence in. But with our new computer and our new friend, Mr. Google, we thought to give it a shot. Most work was done on the weekends, going rather slowly at first as I was still working and driving two hours a day. Esther helped greatly by sanding joints on the new wallboard or painting and varnishing as opportunity arose.

I was greatly privileged to work some number of years through Ciber, one of the more prominent contract agencies in Rochester. In 2006, along with about 20 other Ciber people, I was part of a large project which Ciber was working for Xerox, when Xerox came up with a great idea, supposing the project could be done less expensively by a crew of people from India. Xerox pulled the carpet out from under Ciber, leaving a large number of its employees high and dry.

I was more than a year past standard retirement age, and although I would have loved to continue working, I did not relish the thought of going again through the process of interviewing and coming up-to-speed on a new project. It was time to take my retirement and go home.

Work on the house then became a full-time job for a number of years, as in one room at a time, all lath and plaster walls and ceilings came down, as well as the blown-in insulation behind them. What a dirty job that was.

A new bathroom went in and an oak stairway, wider, longer, replacing the steep one we had climbed for twenty years.

Everything came out of the kitchen, cabinets, appliances, lighting. One of the box stores estimated about $6000 to replace the cabinets. I found a place in Alabama which shipped cabinets, all oak, none of your pasteboard backs and sides. They were shipped in flat boxes. Assembling and hanging them was quite simple. Shipping and all, that expense came to $1700, a sight better than the box stores.

All wiring was replaced down to and including the breaker box. All plumbing came out and new copper plumbing went in. A few

partitions were moved, certain sections of floor and of outer walls were replaced including studs and joists, four steel entry doors were installed and the doorways in most cases moved or widened. Twenty-six new double-paned windows went in with many of them being sized differently than the old ones or placed where none had been, including studs and joists, four steel entry doors were installed and the doorways in most cases moved or widened.

A forty-foot porch was built to replace the old one that had spanned the front of the house and a new roof replaced three layers of old roofing. The roof incidentally, was done by the volunteer labor of friends, people from Beth Israel and my buddies from work. The roof was one detail which I was not willing to take on.

The rented auger came in very handy to sink holes for concrete footings beneath the porch posts. The footings were four feet deep to get below the frost line.

Two layers of wood and asphalt siding were removed from the outside and replaced by new vinyl siding. Here you see three levels of scaffold. It wasn't quite enough so I pulled a step later up top and was just able to touch the peak.

A back corner of the kitchen was dark and good for nothing except to park the refrigerator there. We added four windows, replaced the floor and the joists beneath, and hung a little chandelier above, as shown by the sequence on the next page.

Over the years of work on the house, I received many compliments on the improvements that were taking place but I think the one that meant the most to me came from a busy farmer one day as I

was working at the front of the house. He was driving one of those big tractors that the local farmers used, with eight monster tires, duals on each corner. He came roaring down the road pulling a plow, perhaps a dozen or sixteen plow shares on that piece of equipment with half of the plow folded up onto the other half so it could be towed on the highway.

As the tractor approached my driveway, it suddenly slowed and pulled to the side of the road. The farmer turned off the engine, dismounted and approached me. He introduced himself, and said something like, "I drive this road all the time and have been watching you work on this house. I just felt I needed to stop to compliment you on the beautiful job. I know how hard you have worked and the place looks simply wonderful." He shook my hand, mounted his tractor and roared on down the road.

As we opened up the house to prospective buyers, they would sometimes express surprise at their first sight of the old stone foundation in the basement, having presumed the house to be a new construction. It was a great adventure, a wonderful challenge that all things being equal, I'd do again in a flash.

The Decision

During these years we drove to Florida a few times to visit the off-spring and the new grandchildren. On one of these occasions Donita drove down with us and we stayed at Deanne's place. While there, I was commissioned to build a long book case for her house. I could name Deanne "the commissioner," as she is commissioning me still to this day.

One day as I was working on that project, I began to sense a pain in my back which finally drove me into the house and put me to bed. The pain in my back and leg was excruciating and remained so for many days. It was my first, and I trust it will be my last go-round with sciatica. Thankfully, our good friend, Dr. Kevin Hunger, paid me a visit and prescribed some pain medication which alleviated the pain to some degree. Still it was a most trying time, and also quite demoralizing, as I was confined to bed or couch for more than two weeks. When at last I was able to get to the couch, I laid there and instructed Deanne as she finished the bookcase on the living room floor. She must have done a splendid job, as the bookcase was well used for nearly ten years and then sold for two hundred dollars.

Donita finally had to return to work, and took the car, driving alone back to Rochester. On that day I was left feeling perhaps the lowest I had ever felt in my life.

In a few more weeks I recovered sufficiently that I was able to drive back home in a borrowed car. Thank you, James and Vanessa! By this time, I had made a major decision. Reminding myself of the remote location of our home fifty miles from Donita and from any city of note I decided it was time to sell the house and move south, as the offspring had been encouraging us to do for a number of years. I did not care to have a repeat of sciatica or any other problem with my

Moving Day

health when I lived so far from help. We spent a traumatic winter organizing, boxing, selling or discarding our accumulation of 30 years. My riding lawnmower to which I was attached, even as Dad had been to his big red Farmall tractor in 1950, I now had no further use for, and it stayed with a relative in New York. So much had to go before that big rental truck backed into the front yard on that day in March

of 2011. Wendy Hunger had flown up from Jacksonville and spent the final week helping Esther to pack and prepare for the move. Both Eric and Brian Roes flew up from Jacksonville to help us close out the place. Donita left her job at Shema Yisrael, to the extreme dismay of Rabbi Jim. She brought the furnishings from her apartment and loaded everything onto the truck with our belongings.

We left on a chilly morning in March following a wet snowfall the night before that turned the front lawn into a muddy mess and our truck made it much worse. But for the grace of God we would never have gotten that heavily loaded truck onto the road.

However, with Brian at the wheel and the rest of us in the borrowed car, we arrived at the Rochester Airport. Wendy caught her
plane to Jacksonville just as Juan Sarmiento flew in from Jacksonville. He took the wheel of the rental truck and led the caravan
south. The next 24 hours were tiring but uneventful.

Reaching Jacksonville, we unloaded the truck, most of the load going into a storage facility, a few items into Brian's and Deanne's
house where we were to live initially. After resting up a bit, I returned to the house in New York, rejoining Donita there, as we still
had a remodeling job to complete.

Driving away from our beautiful House.

We worked all day, every day to complete the job. We had porch
and house sales to get rid of much of what was left behind. We still
had doors to finish, baseboard and other trim to be varnished and
installed. Donita's high school friend, Melissa spent many days

160

working with her. We hired a woodworker, Ben Rogers from She-ma Yisrael, to help with installation of the trim, and he spent a couple of weeks working with us. I had a load of topsoil hauled in and dumped on the front lawn which was necessary to fill the ruts made by the truck and smooth out the lawn once again.

So much to do. Amazingly, ten weeks later all was completed. We hung beautiful potted plants across the front of that long porch, said goodbye to the neighbors and to our beautiful new house, turned the key over to the realtor and with very mixed emotions pointed the car south.

I briefly lived in the house once again, about a year later, as it did not sell as rapidly as expected. I got a call from the realtor, saying: "Bad news, Claude. Someone got into your house and stripped out all the copper plumbing." The insurance company reimbursed me quite quickly, and I flew north to go to work again. This time the copper was replaced with PVC. I rented a car and lived in the house for a week or so until all was in order, and then flew back to Jacksonville. In another three or four months the house finally sold and for a price which made us quite happy.

A New Home in Florida

We had arrived! Esther and I lived for a time, a bit more than two years, with Brian, Deanne and the three kids. We were in a fairly sizable house, each having our own wing and having a common living area. I found a few things to do around the place, keeping the lawn mowed, creating some hangers for the instruments in the music room and building a lattice structure over the patio in the back. It was a good time and we are so appreciative of Brian's and Deanne's hospitality. But the owner of our rental house decided to sell, and it seemed a good time to be on our own again.

In June of 2013 we found the perfect little three bedroom rental house in Mandarin, purchased a gently used Toyota for our transportation and made the move.

Our back yard in Mandarin just after we moved in

Newly contoured, patio and planters in place.

At the time we signed our rental contract, I showed the owner a picture of the lattice structure I had built over the patio at the previous residence. She slapped the picture and exclaimed, "You can do that here!" Actually, she told me I could pretty much do as I wished to the property and I have obliged.

My last act at the former location was to keep the lawn mowed for a summer, while the owners were waiting for a sale. For doing that, I was given some very valuable heavy-duty steel shelving, which now stretches for twenty feet along one sidewall of our two-car garage and is so useful for storing much that we still have in boxes.

163

I love having a large garage and have set up a woodshop therein, where I have produced many items for our home, the homes of our offspring, and even to sell. I have a pair of workbenches, one of them being a four-by-eight-foot bench on casters and having a table saw, a miter saw and a jointer inset into the top of the desk so that all work surfaces are level with the bench top.

It was good to settle into our new home in Mandarin. The kitchen and dining room are quite sizable as is the master bedroom. The two smaller bedrooms are well used, one as Esther's sewing room, the other doubling as a guest room and a play room for the grand-kids.

Fortunately, there was room for a laundry tub beside the washing machine so I installed a deep tub there. The fireplace was crying for a mantle, so I built one which is hollow with little trap doors on top

and outlets inside the mantle where lamps or decorations may be plugged in and the cords hidden inside. We have added new lighting and ceiling fans, new outlets both interior and exterior. We now have a lamppost in the frnt lawn and a sidewalk bordering

the driveway. I dug up the entire lawn which was a mess and removed large roots of trees long since gone. I cut down several sizable trees that still were in the lawn, digging out their roots. I recontoured the back yard, built a twelve-by-twenty foot patio, making my own pavers, 625 of them. I poured concrete flowerboxes

around its perimeter and steps leading through them down to the lawn. All of that is now covered with a lattice structure which supports a large American wisteria vine. The recontoured back yard is sodded and turned into an orchard. The house is now surrounded by a dozen citrus trees, and a few others: nectarine trees, mango and fig and olive trees. A chain link fence encloses the back yard and behind it a retention pond which the generous Floridians refer to as a lake. The fence is convenient for the climbing vines of grapes or sweet potatoes planted along its base.

At one side of the back lawn is a large raised bed where our vegetables grow. Out of sight at one end of the house is a chicken yard and coop with a half dozen birds that supply our eggs.

We added some rain gutters, ran all downspouts into drainage tile that I installed underground around the house. The tile runs under the back lawn and discharges our run-off into the "lake."

166

A short time ago I painted the exterior of the house. For some of this activity the landowner reimbursed me or paid for my labor; for some not the case. But we expect to live here for some time and I am investing in our enjoyment for the years ahead.

Esther has been in good health with a few exceptions. She has long had asthma problems, rather severe in days gone-by but quite well controlled of late. The meds are a bit of an expense, a bit over a hundred a month, but would be worse if we did not purchase from an Israeli pharmacy.

Over the last twenty years she has undergone a number of joint replacement operations, two hips, two knees and last year a shoulder replacement. All operations have been very successful and we believe we are doing the economy a huge favor by our support of the titanium industry.

We went through an unsettling period in late 2018 when the landowner told us she needed to sell our house. We began our preparations, at least mental preparations, expecting that we would soon need to make a move. But a friend heard of what was to transpire, stepped in, bought the house before it went on the market and told us it was ours to rent as long as we wished to live there.

We are content where we are, very blessed to be here, and we stay quite busy. All of our "kids" with their spouses and grandkids live within 10 to 30 minutes of our place and all are members and involved in the congregational life of Beth Israel.

An AutoB. that Oughta Be

Early in 2020, I was asked to proof a chapter of an autobiography being written by a gentleman only two or three years older than me, and those pages served as my inspiration and motivator. I promptly began writing pages of my own, cranking out nearly a hundred of them in fact, within the next three weeks. Some may recognize words that you have read elsewhere, as occasionally, I was able to weave in text from a number of shorter items I had previously written.

My assumption as I churned out those pages some months prior to my eightieth birthday was that this would be the end of it, an informal book of sorts, a record that my progeny would appreciate in days to come. I ran off a dozen copies and distributed them to friends who were interested in the read.

To my immense surprise, at my next birthday party I received a gift from my family of those pages bound in a hardcover, assigned a library of congress number, and all looking pretty official. I learned that I was to proof it, add anything I still wished to add, and after meeting with the publisher there was to be a second printing, copies of which would be available to the many people who were already signing up to buy.

The book has grown into three parts, an autobiography, an anthology and an album, all at the insistence of certain trouble-makers whose names I won't reveal, but whose faces appear on the final page of the autobiographical section.

The picture on that final page was made complete within the last half-dozen years by the addition of two new family members; the first of those being Nikita, my youngest grandchild and my last hope for carrying on the Painter name. Thank you for joining our family, Nikita.

And as for the other new member, it happened like this.

Tying it Together

For a number of years, it has been my vision that first-time attenders to our synagogue be given the red carpet treatment as I was the first time I walked through the door at Shema Yisrael. To that end I have served as coordinator of the "Host Team" at Beth Israel.

There are about twenty congenial hosts on our team, people who have a vision similar to my own and for several years there have been five or six of them serving on any Saturday morning, welcoming people into the synagogue.

On one Saturday morning not too long after the Host Team was initiated at Beth Israel, I stood in the lobby saying hello and shaking hands. One gentleman came in whom I had not met before. He had no hair on his head, and I thought now here is an interesting looking guy. I caught his name but did not remember it. I asked him for his name again a week later – and the following week. Why could I not ever recall his name? Little did I know at that time that he was to become my son-in-law.

Donita and Josh: Wedding Day.

Josh and Donita soon discovered each other, the discovery by Josh coming first, and it was not too many months before the announcement was made, a wedding soon followed at Beth Israel, and our family is now complete. Josh is a great addition to the family; the only native Floridian we can claim as our own, and we think the world of him.

Wrapping it Up

We are very thankful for the many good friends that we have in Florida, so many at Beth Israel and also those in the community where we live. We are surrounded by houses where single women live, widowed or divorced or otherwise. I seem to be the go-to neighbor of choice when one thinks she smells smoke in the house or when the garbage disposal goes or a snake is in the back yard or the plumbing develops a leak. Occasionally I help with rather extensive projects such as tiling a bathroom or laying a new floor in a bedroom or dropping a tree or pouring a sidewalk. Esther calls me the neighborhood husband.

Many pages ago you read about our experience at Edgewood Free Methodist Church and an update is very much in order. A few years ago I received a phone call from Jim Appel, still the rabbi at Shema Yisrael. Of course, he knew well of my thoughts and dreams twenty years earlier regarding Edgewood. He called to explain that the church would soon be moving to a larger facility. The pastor and the board of trustees called a meeting with Jim, telling him that they planned to sell their property and wished to see it go to Shema Yisrael. The building had not been made available to anyone else because the

The New Congregation Shema Yisrael!

Edgewood board of trustees and the pastor wanted Shema to have it. They told Jim they would do everything possible to help him and the congregation to make the purchase possible. Incredible.

Since then, things have moved steadily forward. Shema quickly sold its building, remarkable enough but even more so because it was purchased for office use by the very church which once hosted Shema as a fledgling prayer group before it matured into the current Congregation Shema Yisrael.

Contributions and pledges have rolled in to make the Edgewood purchase possible. A closing date was set and met. For a time, the congregation gathered in a temporary location, but even as I am writing this in early December of 2020, it is moving into the new facility and looking forward to occupying the building on this Saturday, December 12. What magnificent timing by our God, and how incredibly appropriate that this first service will also mark the first observation in the new Shema Yisrael of the Hannukah Feast of Dedication.

I would like to think that all the time invested in the Edgewood congregation, the series of classes brought them by the Levines and others from the Shema Yisrael of 25 years ago, that the influence of Rabbi Appel and Randy Katz over the intervening years, all have played a role in sensitizing the Edgewood Congregation to the Lord's design for Rochester's Messianic Community and to its need for this beautiful Messianic Synagogue in this most spectacular location. One thing I surely believe is that God will bless Edgewood Free Methodist Church and those responsible for this contribution to the Kingdom, far more than they could ever have dreamed.

As for Esther and me, it is one more confirmation – one among many, to be sure, – that serving out our lives in the Messianic community is exactly what God had in mind for us. We are so happy, we are so blessed, we are so alive.

That's it, the first 80 years. As for the next 80, all I can say is:

"Bring 'em on!"

The entire clan, 10/17/20:

Back Row:
Brian Roes, Josh and Donita Manning, Deanne and Audrey Roes, Safiya, Anya and Eric Painter.

Front Row:
Brendan Roes, Esther and Claude Painter, Alex Roes.

Down in Front:
Naya and Nikita Painter.

To God be the glory, great things He has done

Part 2. The Anthology

The Willow Tree - Highschool/1958

The willow tree stood modestly
    Beside the rippling rill.
Her every slim and limber limb
    The breezes teased at will.
Her branches looped and swooped and drooped
    A foliaceous train.
The sky grew black, demoniac,
    And laced the earth with rain.
The wind arose and whipped the clothes
    The weeping willow wore;
The little rill began to fill
    Until it spilled ashore.
The thunder crashed; the lightening slashed
    A gash across the sky;
The tempest broke a rigid oak
    And dashed it down to die.
The willow bent. subservient
    Before the brutal blast.
Her branches splayed, she swayed and stayed
    Until the storm was past.

Sand In the Hand
5/15/1959

These lines opened the 1959 Yearbook at the end of my freshman year of school at Spring Arbor College, Michigan.

Between these covers
Lie the stories
Of one of the happiest years
In the lives
Of three hundred people;
The defeats and the victories,
The work and the play,
The hard times and the enjoyable.

Enter
With the Echo Staff of 1959
Through the Golden Door
Of Reminiscence.
Like glistening sand
Melting through your fingers,
Sift the memories
Warmest to you.
As you move
Into the living past
May your enjoyment
Equal ours.

Pies, Pies, Pies
7/9/2017

On Thanksgiving Day our
dining room is oddly
"desserted" with prune
pie, wintergreen pie,
mango pie, starfruit pie...

Pies, pies, pies,
I love your pies,
Apple with cheese,
Pumpkin pie, sure to please.

Raspberry, peach
I will have one of each;
Mincemeat so fine,
Your meringue is divine.

Pies, your pies
Sure take the prize
Filled to my eyes,
Still, there's room for your pies.

Zoo Parade 7/5/2007

The lion is the king of beasts;
He makes an awful roaring noise.
I've heard it said, he often feasts
On naughty little girls and boys.

The rhino is one ugly critter,
Face as ugly as his sitter.
Bigger than a city bus,
That's the ole rhinoceros.

Long and skinny Anaconda
From the river tends to wanda.
'Though he'd dearly love a squeeze,
Best if you don't try to please.

Jungle kitty, that's the cheetah,
Eyes are good and teeth are spiky,
Running faster than your Nike.
He would like you in his pita.

The elephant is big and grey,
He rips up trees when he's at play.
He snatches monkeys with his trunk;
He throws them on the ground, ker-plunk!

Every once upon a while
You may see a crocodile.
Toothy snout and lengthy tail,
When you see him, hit the trail.

The camel, you may well agree,
Is not a pretty sight to see.
His back gives rise to pointy humps,
His face just looks like Grandpa Grumps.

On Turkey Day 11/15/2015

As you sit around your Thanksgiving table this year; lift your voices together to sing these words to the tune of "Oh Christmas Tree."

On turkey day, on turkey day
The family gets together.
It matters not if clouds are grey,
Or inclement the weather.
We gather round the table there
To wait for Dad to say a prayer
While Billy bangs his silverware
And Amy fights with Heather.

The bird reclines in golden brines
And heaps of extra dressing,
And Grandma with the carving knife
Is leaving no one guessing.
She sticks a fork into his chest,
She slices off a steaming test.
She chews and nods, "It is the best!
"It's time to hear the blessing."

The chairs assigned at last, Hurray!
We're seated at the table;
But to Aunt Fay's extreme dismay

Her seat is quite unstable.
It squeaks a lot and moves around,
It makes a problematic sound;
It dumps Aunt Fay upon the ground.
She'll rise again when able.

The chatter goes, it ebbs and flows
It's really worth ignoring;
Aunt Peg is shrill and Uncle Bill
Is rather loud and boring.
The meal was long, I thought I'd die;
At last they brought the pumpkin pie,
We raised our goblets, held 'em high;
But Uncle Bill was snoring.

We played some football in the yard
As fluffy flakes were falling.
And Dad and I played really hard
But Uncle Bill was stalling.
I threw a pass, Dad tipped my throw;
Gramps intercepted, don't you know.
Dad should have blocked but let him go.
The score was most appalling.

The cloudy sky grew darker still,
The sun would soon be setting.
Some pie was left; we ate until
Our tummies were regretting.
The coats came out from off the bed;
The sad good-byes sincerely said.
Aunt Peggy's hand upon my head
I'll not be soon forgetting.

Old-timer's Lament
8/30/2019

Author is unknown; here's hopin' he will not mind a couple of my tweaks.

Long ago and far away, in a land that time forgot,
Before the days of Dylan or the dawn of Camelot,
There lived a race of innocents, of gentle folk and free,
Long ago and far away in a land that fostered me.

Oh, there was truth and goodness in the land where we were born
Where navels were for oranges and Payton Place was porn.
For Ike was in the White House and Hoss was on TV,
And God up in His heaven blessed the land that fostered me.

We longed for love and romance, and we waited for our Prince,
Eddie Fisher married Liz, and no one's seen him since.
We danced to 'Little Darlin,' and sang to 'Stagger Lee'.
And cried for Buddy Holly in a Land that fostered me.

We fell for Frankie Avalon, Annette was oh, so nice,
And when they made a movie, they never made it twice.
We didn't have a Star Trek Five, or Psycho Two and Three,
Or Rocky-Rambo Twenty in the Land that fostered me.

Miss Kitty had a heart of gold, and Chester had a limp,
And Reagan was a Democrat whose co-star was a chimp.
We had a Mr. Wizard, but not a Mr. T,
And Oprah couldn't talk yet, in the Land that fostered me.

We had our share of heroes, we never thought they'd go,
At least not Bobby Darin, or Marilyn Monroe.
For youth was still eternal, and life was yet to be,
And Elvis was forever in the Land that fostered me.

We'd never seen a rock band that was Grateful to be Dead,
And Airplanes weren't named Jefferson, and Zeppelins were not Led.
And Beatles lived in gardens then, and Monkees in a tree,
Madonna – she was Mary in the Land that fostered me.

We'd never heard of microwaves, nor telephones in cars,
And babies might be bottle-fed, but never grown in jars.
And pumping iron got wrinkles out, and 'gay' meant fancy-free,
And dorms were never co-Ed in the Land that fostered me.

We hadn't seen enough of jets to talk about the lag,
And microchips – we found them at the bottom of the bag.
And hardware was a box of nails, and bytes came from a flea,
And rocket ships were fiction in the Land that fostered me.

T-Birds came with portholes, and side shows came with freaks,
And bathing suits came big enough to cover both the cheeks.
And Coke came just in bottles, and skirts below the knee,
And Castro came to power near the Land that fostered me.

We had no Crest with Fluoride, and we had no Hill Street Blues
We had no golden arches, who would want them in his shoes?
There was no patterned pantyhose or Lipton herbal tea
Nor ads for male dysfunctions in the Land that fostered me.

The guys would sport a flat-top, and the gals a pony-tail,
The girls – a pair of earrings, never one upon a male.
And middle-aged was 35 and old was forty-three,
And ancient were our parents in the Land that fostered me.

But all things have a season, or at least that's what they say,
And now instead of Maybelline we swear by Retin-A.
They send us invitations to join AARP,
We've come a long way, baby, from the Land that fostered me.

So now we face a brave new world in slightly larger jeans,
And wonder why they're using smaller print in magazines.
We tell our children's children of the way it used to be,
So long ago, so far away, the Land that fostered me.

Using "Alot" a Lot 1/17/2016

Alot for sale. We speak English here, alot. Sorta.

There's trouble afoot
If you aid and abet
The writer who uses
"Alot" quite a lot.
Examples abound
Of those run amuck
By writing "alot."
One should not.

I warn you anew,
That practice abort.
Such usage, abandon;
I strongly exhort.
You're going afield
Each time you affix
A part where it should
Be apart.

Making Covenant
With Avraham
7/10/2012

An irrevocable covenant.
"As long as the sun shall shine by
day and the moon by night..."

Look north, look south, look east and west,
As far as eye can see.
Get up and walk the length and breadth,
Said Adonai to me.

From Egypt to Euphrates' shore,
I give this land to you,
And to your heirs forevermore,
Inhabit and subdue.

I'll make of you a nation great,
I'll bless you with a birth,
And with descendants as the stars,
And they will bless the earth.

I covenant with you today,
And I will change your name.
I pass between the cow and ram
With fire pot and flame.

You'll wear the sign of covenant,
All males within your land,
This covenant with Adonai
Which shall forever stand.

As long as stars will shine at night
And sun will shine by day,
A covenant with Adonai
Can never pass away.

The Creation 5/14/2017

Seems every culture has a version of the Creation Story. Shucks, I even have one of my own. Perhaps that's because I'm so ancient.

God made the earth in six days flat,
God made the Heavens just like that.
Just like that, in six days flat,
And God said, "This is really good!"
In the beginning all was dark,
God said, "Be light!" and just like that,
There was light, God made Day one,
And God said, "This is really good!"

God made a roof away up high,
Where puffy clouds go floating by.
Made it blue and called it sky,
And God said, "This is really good!"
God put the water in the sea,
God made the land so high and dry,
On Day Two God made the world,
And God said, "This is really good!"

God planted seeds upon the earth,
God planted flowers, grass and trees.
On Day Three God's garden grew,
And God said, "This is really good!"
God made the sun to warm the plants,
God made the moon to shine at night.
On Day Four God made the stars,
And God said, "This is really good!"

God made the fishes in the sea,
God made the birds that sing and fly.
On Day Five God blessed them all,
And God said, "This is really good!"
God made the cattle in the field,
God made the bug and bumble bee.
On Day Six God made them all,
But God still had some work to do.

God made a man to be His friend,
Made man a wife to share their love.
On Day Six God looked and said,
"Now this is really, really good!"
God made the earth in six days flat,
God made it big and round and fat.
On Day Seven God relaxed,
That's how God made the first Shabbat.

The Exodus
A Jewish Coming-out Party.
7/9/2017

A foreshadowing. A remembrance.
"And by His stripes we are healed."

We plowed their fields,
Beneath a burning sun;
We made their bricks
From morn till day was done.
So hard we worked,
So long we carried on.
They whipped our backs;
All hope seemed gone.

We cried to God,
"Remove our heavy load,
The threat of sword,
The pain of lash and goad."
The more we prayed,
The more the whip was plied.
Our burdens grew;
Our children died.

God heard our groans;
He saw us in our grief.
His heart was moved
To bring us sweet relief.
He had a plan
To win our liberty;
To loose the chains
And set us free.

God sent Moshe
To go before the throne;
A humble man,
But he was not alone.
For through this man
God showed His mighty hand,
By wondrous proofs
Throughout the land.

With signs and blood
God brought the Pharaoh down;
Down to the sea
There with his host to drown.
But we prevailed
And traveled through the sea.
By God's strong arm
He set us free.

The Beautiful Jewish Queen 3/10/2016

If you were the only queen in the world
  and I were the only king,
Friends would come to banquet in the royal house,
They would praise the beauty of the royal spouse.
A palace in Shushan waiting for you,
  with servants and everything.
Haman noble counselor to the crown.
Gallant sentries keeping a peaceful town,
If you were the only queen in the world
  and I were the only king,

A garden in Persia made just for two,
  made just for a king and queen.
Treachery comes calling; Mordecai's aware;
Brings the scheme to light and saves the kingship there.
A note in the log book, Mordecai's name
  is seen by a grateful king,
Mordechai rides high on the royal steed
Led by Haman just as the king decreed,
With Haman announcing, "Here is the man
  regarded so well by the king."

The king promised Esther half of the realm;
     not sure if he said just when.
Wait, what does he hear about a scheming plan?
Who would want to do away with Esther's clan?
A stunning surprise, the queen is a Jew
     and Haman would purge her kin.
Esther bravely goes to inform the crown,
Risks her life while knowing she might go down.
She enters the throne room, kneels to the king,
     he beckons the queen, come in.

Our beautiful Esther spilled all the news,
     and surely it riled the king.
Haman pays the price for such extreme abuse,
Finds himself suspended from his own hemp noose.
The king's new decree set all the Jews free
     to do that resistance thing.
Esther keeps her title as favored queen,
Now we dress each year like it's Halloween,
Recalling the Jewish queen of the realm
     confronting the Persian king,

A song for Purim: these lines can be (and have been) sung to the tune of "IF You Were the Only Girl in the World," as rendered in the first verse of this recording by the amazing Buffalo Bills Barbershop Quartet.

https://www.youtube.com/watch?v=yBwDChwHHFc

Maker of Time, Master of Days 12/16/2011

He makes all things beautiful in his time.

Who sets the sun ablaze in the height?
Who spins the earth from night into light?
Who marks the seasons; the Spring and the Fall?
Adonai, Maker of Time, does it all.

When it was time, Who worked out a plan?
When it was time, first the earth, then a man.
When it was time, satisfaction expressed,
Adonai, Master of Days, took a rest.

When it as time, Who parted the sea?
Adonai surely; who else could it be?
When it was time, Who offered a ram?
Adonai, Savior, "I am who I am."

When it was time, Who halted the sun?
Adonai did; Adonai was the One.
When it was time, Who toppled the wall?
Adonai, Mighty One, Master of all.

When it was time, Who guided a Star?
Heralded shepherds, brought men from afar?
When it was time, Who gave us a King?
Adonai, Adonai worked everything.

When it was time, A blood-spattered tree;
When it was time, A life spent for me.
When it was time, A stone rolled away;
Adonai risen, He only, could pay.

When it was time, having said His goodbye,
Adonai Son sits with Father on high.
When it is time, He'll return with His own,
Adonai reigns for ALL time from His throne.

Never too early and never too late,
His timing is perfect. Perhaps I must wait.
He orders my footsteps; I walk in His Ways:
Maker of Time and the Master of Days.

Reading – Vignettes
2/21/2008

Read a book, even a dog-eared one on these dog days of summer.

Today was the day I began unloading the boxes of books that I had stored while my study was being remodeled. It was like living my life over again, and it is responsible for this download from the databanks.

The books brought back memories of stories from my younger days and I decided to pass them on to the rest of the family. I think I may do that now and then, when something comes to mind, and before Alzheimer's sets in. Otherwise, you may never fully comprehend what a fruitcake your old man was as a young man.

Vignette 1 - The day I discovered reading:

I attended 2nd and 3rd grades in a one room country school house, with only one other student, (a boy, thank goodness,) in my grade. I was a good reader, but saw reading as something to fill the time, when there was nothing better to do. Since the teacher taught grades K through 8, I often had spare time on my hands, so would go to the single book case in the room, to look for a book that I hadn't already memorized.

One day, desperate, I picked up a book which I had always rejected before because it was so small, black, with fine print and no pictures. None! Not much of a book by my standards. But I sat down at my seat and began my first adventure with a classic, Treasure Island. It was incredible. I was riveted. I was forever changed. For two days I could hardly eat or sleep. That was the day I learned what reading is really all about.

Vignette 2:

I was perhaps fourteen when one day I was invited to the home of an elderly lady from our church, who had many books and who thought I might find some of interest among them. I was invited to help myself. What an afternoon I had going through the bookcases and boxes in her attic; I thought I'd died and gone to Heaven. I don't know what my dad thought when I brought those boxes of books home, but I'm sure Mom was delighted. I probably have every one of those books yet, many of them sitting on the shelves behind me, as I write.

Vignette 3:

In 7th and 8th grade we students were given a monthly paper, from Scholastic Magazine or something, from which we could select inexpensive paperbacks that the teacher would order for us. What an exciting time each month when the teacher distributed that paper, and I went through, reading the blurbs and checking off all the "must have" books, doing my best to temper my appetite, knowing the wrath of my father that I would have to endure. He could not afford a box of paperbacks every month.

Of course, I put my order in first, so there was no going back. Then I explained to Dad that I really needed these 12 or 15 books, and they were very cheap adding up to only X number of dollars which I needed to have by next Monday. In the end, he always came through, and on the day when those books arrived, I knew it was worth it all. Again, those paperbacks today fill a long shelf on the wall behind my chair. Thanks, Dad. You always cane through.

AM's IMAX 7/24/2015

We spent a couple of wonderful hours in front-row lawn chairs last night, wife and I, sitting just inside the raised door of the garage enjoying God's mighty media center, with the evening's entertainment being a spectacular panoramic presentation of nature's brawny elements at their finest.

Rain blew in slanted sheets across the screen before us, eroding earth, ricocheting off roadway, pelting, splashing, stabbing, slashing, forming little streams which soon became tributaries and were then absorbed into the pools they created. An occasional misty wave blew through the doorway, giving us a sense of inclusion in the display and feeling most refreshing after the hundred-degree temperature of three hours ago.

There was the light show in original IMAX technology, the brilliant bolts crisscrossing the sky and driving their jagged shafts into the ground, their intense strobe effect betraying moss-shrouded trees reeling like drunken sailors before the wind.

No less spectacular was the audio component of this multi-media extravaganza, the voices of those saw-toothed streaks as they linked heaven and earth, voices out of sync with those dazzling jagged barbs but which were inevitably to follow, voices ranging from the distant deep rolling basses through the less remote baritone sections rich in surround sound to the violent ear-splitting crack of one or another top tenor, always anticipated yet always startling, always seeming to be just around the corner.

What magnificent pageantry. And all for free.

And when at last it was over.....

Appalachian Vacation – 12/26/2011

It was the summer of 1966. I was 25, free as a bird for a week or two, enjoying a footloose vacation in my little '65 Triumph Spitfire.

Navigating the steep hills and sharp curves of the Appalachians, wandering over the torturous back roads of Kentucky, I made an impulsive decision to attend the Sunday morning service about to begin in a tiny one-room church nestled among the hills.

There were perhaps twenty people in attendance, singing lustily, following the words which the pastor lined out to them from the only hymn book in the building. Following the music, Sister Ruth was called upon for an impromptu testimony, responding enthusiastically and at considerable length.

Came time for the offering, and the pastor made an impassioned plea for a little extra from his parishioners, something that might be applied to their outstanding mortgage, a figure that had been hanging over their heads for some time. The figure, it turned out, was twenty dollars.

In those days I didn't have a charge card to my name or a lot of cash on hand either, so it was a concern that I not run out of twenties before returning home. Even so, I deposited one of them into the basket as it came by, never dreaming that the offering would be counted while we sang the next song, and the amount immediately reported back to the little congregation.

Following the song, the usher informed the pastor from the back of the room, "Twenty-one dollars and thirty-seven cents."

The pastor responded, "Praise the Lord. One dollar and thirty-seven cents."

The usher raised his voice to say, "Pastor, that was TWENTY-one dollars and thirty-seven cents."

The pastor seemed confused for a moment. Then he began to really praise the Lord. "First thing in the morning, I'll be going to the bank to clear off that mortgage!"

Following the message, a happy congregation greeted the obvious source of the unexpected contribution, and the pastor invited me to his place for lunch. We talked at length over a can of spam until I said my goodbye and crawled into my little roadster.

As I disappeared over the hill and around the next curve I could still see in my rearview, a happy penniless pastor standing by the road and waving at my cloud of dust.

Ogden Nash 1/16/1967
Assignment for Linguistics Class:
"Oral interpretation of Literature"

Ogden Nash loves words. He professes to have that love; he demonstrates it and demonstrates it. He can compress a world of experience into a four-word nutshell, as he did when he wrote:

"The Bronx?
No thonx!"

Or he can stretch his lines on and on and on...

"Well, he was driving on his new tires at 25 miles an hour in the left-hand lane of a dual highway last week, was Mr. Sohwellenbach,
And a car coming the other way owned by a loan shark who had bought his old tires cheap had a blowout and jumped the dividing line and knocked him to hellenbach."

Nash says that his style of squeezing an amazing number of metric feet into a single line is a cover-up for his "half-baked" literacy. He has been referred to as an assassin of poetry. His rhymes are out of this world. He teases and tortures, he bends and brakes, he creates new words and stamps on the old ones. He takes time to give an explanation in his "Brief Guide to Rhyming:"

English is a language than which none is sublimer,

But it presents certain difficulties for the rhymer.
There are no rhymes for orange or silver,
Unless liberties you pilfer.
I was once slapped by a young lady named Miss Goringe,
And the only reason I looked at her that way, she represented a rhyme for orange.
I suggest that some painter do a tormented mural
On the perversity of the English plural.
Because perhaps the rhymer's greatest distress
Is caused by the letter, "s."
Oh, what a tangled web the early grammarians spun!
The singular verb has an "s" and the singular noun has none.
The rhymer notes this fact and ponders without success on it,
And moves on to find that his plural verb has dropped the "s" and his plural noun has grown an "s" on it.
Many a budding poet has abandoned his career,
Unable to overcome this problem that while the ear hears, the ears hear.
Yet he might have had the most splendiferous of careers
If only the "s's" came out even and he could tell us what his ears hears.
However, I am happy to say that out from the bottom of this Pandora's box there flew
A butterfly; not a moth,
The darling four-letter word d-o-t-h which is pronounced "duth" although here we pronounce it "doth."
Pronounce? Let jubilant rhymers pronounce it loud and clear,
Because when they can't sing that their ear hear, they can legitimately sing that their ear doth hear.

Nash thinks of his works as "comments in verse," rather than poetry. His commentary must say something, no matter how minor that something might be. Once he observed:

The turtle lives twixt plaited decks
Which practically conceal its sex.

I think it clever of the turtle
In such a fix to be so fertile.

As one writes and writes and writes, he produces an autobiography, of sorts. Nash was a bachelor when his first book was published. When the second one came out, he was a participant in a brang-spang new marriage. He continued to write as a father – and now as a grandfather he writes in this fashion:

My grandchild who when walking, wobbles,
Calls dogs bow-wows and turkeys gobbles.
Today I called a cow, Moo-moo.
She's got me talking that way, too.

If ever the grandkids wear Ogden down, he can always retire to that other lyric haunt so dear to his heart, animal-land. He is the tender of an entire poetic zoo. Here are a few of the animals kept within his literary cages.

The ostrich roams the great Sahara,
Its mouth is wide, its neck is narra.
It has such long and lofty legs,
I'm glad it sits to lay its eggs.

In the world of mules,
There are no rules.

I've never seen an abominable snowman,
I'm hoping not to see one;
I'm also hoping, if I do,
That it will be a wee one.

And so on.

Often Nash turns his verbal acrobatics, his metric sometimes-feet-sometimes-chaos into a satirical tool to tell us of his pet peeves.

Anything can come under his poetic probe: automobile or air travel, breakfast or the Bronx, coffee served with the meal or censorship of the critics.

In one of his such poems, we get another glimpse of Nash. Though he takes such great liberty with words, though he uses them in ways they have been used never once before, he feels there are still ways not to use them. In the following poem he strikes out at those who misuse our language, those who violate the old conventional rules of grammar. Listen to him, the man called an assassin of words, as he tells us, "Oafishness sells good like an advertisement should."

I guess it is farewell to grammatical compunction,
I guess a preposition is the same as a conjunction,
I guess an adjective is the same as an adverb.
And "to parse" is a bad verb.
Blow, blow, thou winter wind.
Thou art not that unkind.
Like man's ingratitude to his ancestors who left him the English language for an inheritance;
This is a chromium world in which even the Copley Plazas and the Blackstones and the Book Cadillacs are simplified into Sheratons.
I guess our ancient speech has gone so flat that we like to spike it;
Like the hart panteth for the water brooks, I pant for a revival of Shakespeare's "Like You Like It."
I can see the tense draftees relax and purr
When the sergeant barks, "Like you were."
-- And don't try to tell me that our well has been defiled by immigration.
Like goes Madison Avenue, Like so goes the nation.

Long live Ogden Nash!

Lances of South American Indians

Blind Date 8/16/1961

The winter of 1961-62, about the midpoint of my Air Force Language Institute experience at Syracuse University, I desperately needed a break in the action. I learned that the Blackwood Brothers and other southern style gospel quartets were scheduled for an All-Night Hymn Sing, as they were called in those days, to be held in Detroit on the Saturday evening of my long anticipated three-day weekend.

I was able to contact one of my old Spring Arbor College buddies (who shall remain nameless because I can no longer remember who it might have been,) and persuade him to meet me in Detroit for that event with a carload of Spring Arbor guys, and their dates. One additional requirement I laid upon him, was that this carload was to include a date for me, as well.

All went well on the Saturday of the event. I drove all day, from Syracuse to Detroit, and met my Spring Arbor friends at Cobo Hall, that evening. To be sure, I was a bit disappointed with the blind date presented me, and really did not behave as gentlemanly as I might have, throughout the evening. Once introduced, I promptly forgot her last name, but no matter, or so I supposed. I was again with my friends, and I loved that southern style gospel singing. It was a great evening, until about 2:00 AM, when the "All Night Sing" came to an end, Blackwoods and Statesmans sharing the stage for a final song, a male octet rendition that caused the pillars to vibrate and nearly brought the house down.

It was then that I learned, the home of my date was roughly halfway between Detroit and Spring Arbor, and her parents were expecting to host the entire party at their home, overnight. Oh, boy. Well, probably a good idea, since I was exhausted after a day of driving and a night of hand-clapping. I was so sleepy that I could hardly keep the car on the road until we reached her home.

We arrived, and I could not believe the anthropological dream that awaited, as we walked into the home of my date, a house having walls covered with carved wooden masks, spears standing in the corners, and seemingly no end to this display of wonders gathered from the aboriginal ends of the earth.

I stumbled into bed, and slept the sleep of the dead, but was the first of our party to tumble out, the next morning. I found "Mom" alone in the kitchen, working on our breakfast. I could not wait to interrogate her regarding these amazing items all around me, but got no further satisfaction than, "Oh just a few things we picked up in our travels."

I wandered around the house examining artifacts and pictures, and thinking back on my days even before Spring Arbor College, when I was so intrigued by missionary stories, especially by such books as "Words Wanted," and "2000 Tongues to Go." Those books had sparked a real interest in linguistics, and were in no small measure the reason behind my current enrollment in the Air Force Russian Language program.

I reflected on a trip I had made several months ago, returning from a Michigan vacation to my base in Texas, and engineering a side trip to Oklahoma University that I might spend 24 hours visiting the Summer Institute of Linguistics in session there. What an incredible experience it was to sit in those classes, observing those budding linguists interacting with American Indians, learning to learn exotic languages, reducing strange sounds to phonetic symbols and again reproducing those sounds now recorded in their notebooks.

What an experience to listen to a presentation highly anticipated by these student missionaries, a riveting lecture given by Dr. Kenneth Pike, early member of Wycliffe Bible Translators and longtime president of the Summer Institute of Linguistics, as he reviewed a book called "Flatland." Flatland was a two-dimensional world, in which lived a two-dimensional individual who Dr. Pike referred to as "Flatlander." Dr Pike explained how Flatlander had somehow made contact with an inhabitant of a three-dimensional world. He related Flatlander's exceedingly difficult attempt to comprehend this three-dimensional person, this additional dimension, this new world, thereby illustrating to his audience of future translators the immensity of the problem one faces in crossing a cultural line, as is so critical in translating the Bible into a new and exotic culture.

As I stood there looking at lances and arrows and photographs of Ecuadorian Indians, as all these memories were washing over me, at last, at last, the pieces snapped into place. "Words Wanted," authored by Eunice Pike, "Flatlander" the lecture of Dr. Kenneth Pike. I knew Dr. Pike was a professor of linguistics at the University of Michigan in Ann Arbor. We had just slept the night in Ann Arbor.

That is when I remembered the name of my blind date, niece of author Eunice Pike, daughter of linguist Dr. Kenneth Pike, Spring Arbor coed — Barbara — Pike.

Back in the Day 8/31/2017

For many of us who grew up Free Methodist much of the wonder of that experience was in the bonds we developed with one or another of our amazing high schools and colleges. And if your experience was anything like mine, the first loop of those bonds was thrown 'round you by one of those magnificent college male quartets that came to sing in our churches, at our youth camps and on our conference grounds, back in the day.

As though it were yesterday, I remember East Michigan Conference in the summer of 1957, and the thrill of singing in the choir next to that bass from the Spring Arbor quartet. I could never have imagined that a year later I would be singing in his shoes.

The summer of 1958 was the summer of the Ambassador Quartet. Oh, I know there were many other summers with other Ambassador Quartets. But this Ambassador Quartet was special because its members were Ed Slater, Mark Mason, Gordon Evoy and Claude Painter. Three of these are now singing with the angels so it is left to me to relate the untold story which follows.

Our first gig of the summer was the rustic Alpena District Camp Meeting away up north in Michigan. Since we had a couple of weeks to kill between the end of school and the beginning of camp, we remained on campus, employed in such enjoyable activities as painting stuff and cleaning ovens. "Someone" thought of a great idea. Why not ride bicycles to our first camp? It was only a bit more than 200 miles and we had a week to make the trip. So, it was decided.

Of course, we didn't have bikes but no matter. There were a number of local individuals who did, and who loaned them to us. Old refrigerator shelves made great supports wired on the eight fenders. They needed to be well attached to support our sleeping bags and hammocks, our pots for cooking, our food, our clothing including suits for the week of camp. Two weeks of living was bundled up on those eight refrigerator grates.

These bicycles, three of them anyway, were the old-fashioned heavy sort with the wide rubber tires. We were to take turns riding those and the one new-fangled bike having narrow wheels and a gear shift with three gears. Unfortunately, that gear shift was dysfunctional and required a full day of attention before it was finally made reliable. That day cut severely into our travel time; nonetheless we wanted to get on the road before the day was gone. So, at about 6:00 PM on a Monday night, our adventure began.

We biked about five miles before night fell and some rain fell with it. In the vicinity of – was it Parma? – we called it a day, found an old barn, and rolled out our sleeping bags in the hay. It was a long and chilly night, particularly for Ed who had the hammock. But we were on our way and from that point the Ambassadors pedaled about 50 miles a day.

However, we modified our modus operandi following that first chilly evening. Now we always managed to swing by a Free Methodist parsonage sometime in the late afternoon, and stop for a little visit with the pastor and family. "We're the Ambassadors, How d'you do, d'you do?" Surprisingly they always invited us to join them for the evening meal. So, we would sing for our supper, supposing that to be the least we could do. Next would be an invitation to use the shower (big surprise...) and we would then be bedded down for the night. It was a brilliant strategy and a no-fail system.

Up and at 'em the next morning. A solid breakfast and we were on the road. The roads we traveled were two lane roads, (not that there

There are so many hills to climb upward,
I often am longing for rest,
But He who appoints me my pathway
Knows just what is needful and best.
I know in His word He has promised
That my strength, "it shall be as my day"
And the toils of the road will seem nothing
When I get to the end of the way.

was much else in Michigan in 1958,) and usually they did not have a lot of traffic to contend with. As we traveled farther north the land became quite quite hilly. Sometimes those hills seemed to go up forever but interestingly the other side seemed never to be nearly so long. It was then that this verse written by Charles Tillman came to mind.

On one occasion we stopped for a Coke at a little Mom 'n' Pop store away out in the boonies. We stood around in the little building talking with the elderly Mom 'n' Pop tending the store, and then offered to sing them a song. Certainly, they didn't expect the sort of music they heard that day. Together they stood behind the counter weeping as we exhausted our repertoire.

By the end of the third full day – or was it the fourth – we had reached Rose City, a friendly little dot on the map, noted primarily for the artesian well by the side of the road where travelers often stopped to slake their thirst and stretch their legs. Thankfully, Rose City also had a little Free Methodist Church by the side of the road, which was pastored at that time by "Sister Booth," a friendly former pastor of mine who was now widowed but still carrying on with her calling. Sister Booth gave us the usual treatment. I hope her pastorate added a little bonus to her paycheck in restoration of that which the locusts devoured as we passed through.

The next morning as we were about to set out on the final 50 miles of our adventure, we were greeted by a pickup truck and a car driven by cousins of mine who lived near our destination. They had heard that we were in the area and they came looking for us. It was in my considered opinion a rather inglorious conclusion to our great adventure as we loaded the bikes into the back of the pickup. But as we followed that narrow black ribbon up and down the hills and through the dark pines to our destination, it began to seem not such a bad idea after all.

The weekend ahead was great R&R following which we were able to climb the steps to the platform to sing on Monday night. I'm not so sure we could have done that two days earlier.

Dad with his pickup retrieved the four bikes and returned them to Spring Arbor. On my next visit there, I removed the refrigerator shelves and rode the bikes to their various owners. Well, let's say I rode three bikes to their various owners. But that skinny-wheeled bike that served so faithfully for 200 miles, wouldn't you know: when I mounted that bike - the gear shift broke.

The Wedding
8/10/2012
Honeymoon Suite

Classic Metzendorf camper produced in the 50's by
Martin Metzendorf of West Farmington, Ohio

On June 18, 1967, Esther Holiday and Claude Painter were united in holy matrimony. The big question which this composition will try to answer, is what led up to that prominent point in time, that eventual event in their lives, and what can be told about their wedding and the honeymoon which followed. This is that story.

Esther was the eldest of five children, and had been away from her family for several years as she was attending school. Her younger siblings still lived with their parents and Grandma Slaughter, in Fruitland, Idaho near the border with Oregon. Esther in 1966, when our story begins, was a lonely biology major at Roberts Wesleyan College in North Chili, New York.

About 10 miles north of the college was an intersection known as Parma Corners, and at that intersection a rickety wood frame building, 150 years old with a weatherworn sign labeling it as the Parma Free Methodist Church. Claude and his younger sister, Lois, had left the home of their youth, their parents and sister, in Durand, a village of 3000 in south central Michigan, coming to western New York to attend college and to find work. They now attended the old church at Parma Corners and lived in a rented farmhouse just two doors away. Between the old farmhouse and the rickety church sat the parsonage, another old frame construction wherein lived the pastor and his family.

Esther and Claude had some friends in common: Darlene Reiman and her two brothers who attended Roberts Wesleyan during the week, and the little Parma Free Methodist Church on the weekend. It was Darlene who invited Esther to attend the Parma church with her one Sunday, and it was she who introduced Claude and Esther to each other that summer morning in 1966. Claude and Esther took it from there.

Darlene was in matchmaker mode, bringing three couples together that summer of '66. She paid a price for such activity, as in the summer of '67, she was traveling about the country fulfilling her obligation to attend the weddings of those same three couples. One of those weddings was of course, Esther's and Claude's.

But in that summer of '66, Esther was working on campus to make a few dollars. Claude had been working midnight to eight at Kodak and taking 12 hours per semester, 6 per summer session at Brockport, a state university college near Rochester. Still they found time to get acquainted. For their first official date, they went to see the Hill Cumorah Pageant, an enormous extravagant annual outdoor spectacle presented on the hillsides near Palmyra, New York, a depiction by the Church of Latter-Day Saints of its early history, or at least the good parts of its early history. One might argue, not such a romantic beginning, but a spectacular spectacle it was, and it was a fun first time together.

Claude learned that Esther was the firstborn of the five, and daughter of a scholarly book-loving Free Methodist pastor who was then filling a hard-scrabble circuit in Idaho, and working as a common farm laborer to support his family. Besides the family of five kids, a grandmother lived with them, occasionally even two grandmothers – and a cat named Joe Cool. It was not until months later when he visited her home that he could appreciate their modest quarters and the sacrificial lifestyle required of her family due to her father's call to the ministry. It was then that Claude saw throughout the house, the furniture that Dad had built, dressers, tables, the boys' homemade bunks with rope net supporting their mattresses. But that visit was almost a year away.

Claude asked Esther for a second date, a bit more audacious than the first, but she agreed. They drove to Michigan, eight hours each way, for the weekend. Both of them being of Free Methodist lineage, it seemed appropriate to Claude, to visit his family as they were camping at the annual camp meeting of the East Michigan Conference. This yearly event was a time when perhaps 2500 people from 100 churches came together for two weeks, and it had been an important highlight in Claude's summers as he was growing up. Many were the friends and relatives who were there on that weekend; it was the perfect time to introduce them to Esther, and she to them.

It soon became clear to Claude that Esther was the right one for him; and fortunately, she quickly came to hold a reciprocal opinion. They soon were engaged, the phone call was made to Idaho to request and obtain the official buy-in from Esther's papa, (sight unseen,) and the deal was clinched with – not the standard engagement ring, mind you, but a new Singer sewing machine for Esther. That departure from the standard convention produced returns for nearly 50 years and was perhaps the best investment the groom ever made, second only to the bride, herself.

The school year wore on, a bit slowly it seemed at times; more trips to Michigan at Thanksgiving and again at Christmas. With a wedding coming up, Claude again dropped out of school for the spring semester, and picked up a second full time job, working 80 hours a week, often more, until Esther's graduation.

In the spring of '67, Esther graduated from Roberts Wesleyan with a major in biology. Her mother came from Idaho to see Esther walk the stage and claim her sheepskin, and to find out who was this guy to whom her daughter had become so attached. Following graduation, the three of them drove to Idaho in a brand-new blue Chevy, towing and living in a newly purchased 13-foot Amish-built hardtop camping trailer. The ladies slept in the trailer at night, while Claude had his own private quarters in the car. They took time to visit a few national sites on the trip west, Craters of the Moon and Mt. Rushmore among them, but the main focus was on reaching the final destination.

They eventually reached Fruitland, Payette County, Idaho, and following a frantic week of preparations were married there in the little Free Methodist Church, on Sunday afternoon, June 18, 1967. It was a wedding on a shoestring, and a thin shoestring at that, but one that was long remembered by the local citizenry in attendance. There were lots of flowers which came not from a florist shop, but from the local gardens of friends. There was lots of special music for the wedding, which came entirely from the wedding party.

Claude's family drove from Michigan for the wedding, of course. His sister, Lois, was one of the bridesmaids, as were Mary, Esther's sister, and Shanna who would soon become Jim's bride. Jim was best man, his brothers, David and Sam were the ushers. The ushers seated mothers and guests until taking their places next to Jim's station. Jim, however, moved from his place to the minister's place behind the alter, as the ceremony began. Preparing for the ministry, Jim got his first experience officiating, until the bride's father delivered the bride to the alter. At that point, Jim reassumed his place as best man, and Rev. Dad Holiday took over to finish officiating at the wedding.

Regarding the music, Jim sang a solo at one point in the ceremony, as did Lois. The groom sang "The Lord's Prayer," and the bride joined him to sing "Savior Like a Shepherd Lead Us." For that duet, the bride's mother left her seat of honor to accompany on the organ.

High point of the reception was a beautiful wedding cake made by one of the local women. Wedding and reception, both were a resounding success, the bride was beautiful, the dress was gorgeous, the guests were happy and the gifts were numerous.

The couple enjoyed a few days of anonymity in Boise, honeymoon hotspot and tumbleweed capital of Idaho. Details which can be shared: Claude got a speck of something in his eye which required a visit to a doctor. The offensive particle was removed and Claude wore an eyepatch around Boise. The honeymooners enjoyed a day at the well-known Boise Zoo, well known locally, not so much on a national level, but no matter. They still share fond memories of the friendly elk following them along the fence, eventually draining Claude's entire bottle of Dr. Pepper, as it was poked through the wire.

The newlyweds returned to the Holiday home in Fruitland to load the wedding presents into the little Amish house trailer, to say their thankyous and goodbyes and to begin the long trek back to New York. Driving north through Montana and Glacier National Park, they passed by snow banks still melting along the roadside in late June, and crossed into Canada. Route 1, the major route spanning Canada, stretched on endlessly, so it seemed, with but one event memorable enough to be remembered.

It was late at night, a dark, moonless night with Esther at the wheel, pulling the trailer between walls of tall pine trees and around a sharp curve where suddenly a bear appeared in the headlights. The car was moving at a very good speed and there was no way one could have stopped in time. Somehow Esther managed to whip the speeding car and its trailing payload, around that big black blob without touching him, and the newlyweds continued on their way. Surely there were angels surrounding them on that night.

They crossed out of Canada into Michigan, crossed the long bridge spanning the Straits of Mackinac, and continued south to Claude's parents' home in central Michigan. It was a happy arrival, a very happy arrival in fact, since the gas tank was nearly empty and the billfold entirely so. In those days one didn't carry a pocket full of plastic. Dad loaned Claude a few dollars to complete the trip home, and without further adventure they crossed Ontario, arriving at their new home not far from Parma Corners, just in time to return to work the next Monday.

It had been a lovely wedding, a wonderful time, a great adventure, but little did they know how the adventure would pale in the days ahead, pale in comparison to the adventures they would yet experience in the months and years to come.

Dad – Fathers' Day 6/15/2016

Fathers' Day. I found myself reflecting a bit today about my own father, born 1907, the seventh of nine raised on a farm carved from the woods of a rough and tumble northern Michigan. A poor farm boy who began early to cultivate the fields behind a team of horses, a farm boy who attended a one room country school house for only the few months between harvest season and the next planting time, and even that through only the fourth grade, Dad's childhood dream of becoming a doctor was beyond unattainable.

I remember him from my own childhood days as a man strong and tough as rocks, standing tall in my eyes, only later to realize that 5 feet 2 inches was not really so tall. I remember him working like a dog to provide for his wife and two kids,  farming two hundred acres of cropland, and managing a herd of twenty Holstein milkers with the primitive milking equipment of the day. I remember him carrying five-gallon buckets through sucking mud or drifts of snow, two buckets at a time of that frothy white gold; carrying it across the barnyard to the cement block milk house and pouring it through the strainer into the big milk cans for pickup later in the day.

I remember him changing into fresh clothes to drive to the nearby town where he worked a 45 hour week in a small factory. I remember him returning home to "do the chores" again before mounting the big red "H" Farmall and roaring down the lane to plow or cultivate by tractor light. But I do not remember because I was asleep at eleven o'clock, when he would return to the house for four or five hours of rest before arising to do it all over again.

But Sunday, except for doing the chores, was a different day. All else was put on hold as Dad, faithful as sunup, would drive his family to the nearby town where we always attended church, not just once, but a second time in the evening. Only the vilest blizzard or ice storm would disrupt that routine and I have almost no memory of ever missing a service.

As one might expect, Dad eventually sought relief from his unrelenting lifestyle, left the farm life he had always known and moved his young family into the small town. Even so, the farm did not leave Dad, and although he sold everything else at that auction, he could not part with the Farmall. He brought it to town and for years continued renting a few fields on the outskirts of the village. The neighbors were often amused to see Dad following a day's work in the shop, sitting high on his red Farmall, roaring down the streets of the little town on his way to work those fields for the planting of wheat or corn.

In time, Dad began a business of his own which no longer made him a slave to the clock. And although the work was hard, hot in the summer and often bitter in the Michigan winter, it was his baby, it provided well, and he was happy. As I grew older, leaving home, becoming preoccupied with the college experience and the years in the military, inevitably Dad didn't occupy quite the same place in my life that he once had, and I was the loser for that.

But the work ethic that he taught by his example, his undying commitment to his family and to the things that are most important in life, his love for us (although that is not a word he would have easily used,) that is something I never lost. Those lessons have meant so much to me across the years, and have mightily influenced my own path and the way I raised my own family.

Now as an old man, (but not THAT old,) I find it so rewarding to see Dad's influence extended yet another generation into the families of my offspring, and although I may not hang around for generations still to come, I still expect a bit of Dad to filter down... Thanks, Dad, you were the best.

Camp Meetin' 12/18/2012

"Tabernacle" on the campground
of the East Michigan Conference.

As I was growing up in the late 40's and 50's, annual camp and conference in our East Michigan Conference was a big deal and certainly one of the high points of the year. There was a 40-acre camp site with many little cottages and lots of space *filled* with tents and trailers of campers from across the state. Camp meeting for the two largest districts, Flint and Lansing, was a week in length, and immediately followed by a week of conference when the current campers were joined by folks from the three other districts, Port Huron, Bay City and Alpena. As we lived in the Flint District, and only about twenty miles from the campground, we would set up a tent and move (refrigerator and all,) to the camp ground for the entire two weeks. Dad could still work at his job during the day, and drive in to spend the overnight at camp. The second week was especially exciting, as my roots, meaning my cousins, were part of the Alpena District, and many of the relatives would make the 200-mile trek south to become part of the camp during that week. What a glorious two weeks it was.

Services were held in a large rustic "tabernacle" which would seat 2000 or more, and in which the floor in my earliest memory was spread with fresh, delicious smelling wood chips and shavings, making the lengthy periods spent on 8 year old knees much more tolerable than they were to become once the cement floor was in place. Between the pillars in the side walls were doors roughly eight feet square, hinged at the top, which opened out and up, supported in a horizontal position by drop down poles at the outer corners, offering protection from sun and rain for many more people sitting in their folding chairs just outside the foundations.

But the best part of the tabernacle was the little book store at the back wall. Most of the week, except when a service was in session, the doors, again hinged at the top, would be open to the long counter spread with white sheets which hung low behind, and on which was spread a mind-boggling array of colorful books, books for boys like the Sugar Creek Gang series, books about missionaries to Peru or to headhunters of the Amazon, and about anything else one could imagine. For two weeks I lived there.

I used to snitch one of those books when the salesman wasn't looking, sneak around behind and beneath the counter, to sit on the floor behind those low-hanging sheets and read for hours. Of course, the salesman (one of our Free Methodist pastors,) knew full well what was going on, but he always knew when to look the other way. Even then, I was pretty sure that he knew about me, because he always knew to stoop down, raise the sheet, and tell me when it was closing time. I'm also pretty sure that God has a really special place reserved for him.

On Conference Sunday morning, all the stops were pulled out, as the pastors of the conference, more than 100 of them, were seated on the huge platform that spanned the front of the tabernacle. For many people, the high point of the service was a riveting message by the bishop that would have them weeping or shouting at its conclusion.

For me, the high point was a song or two rendered by a male quartet, four students from Spring Arbor College. It didn't occur to me at the time, that one day I might be standing up there, singing with the male quartet from Spring Arbor.

But among those impressive rows of pastors on the platform, there was one who always stood out above the rest, in my young memory. He was an elderly gentleman, tall, straight as a ramrod, entirely at ease before 2000 people, and often standing at the microphone. I had no idea who he was, or what was his name, only that he was impressive in his stature, his bearing, and most of all by that white clerical collar he wore with his black suit, rather than a tie such as was worn by any other pastor I had ever seen. I didn't understand that collar. It made no sense to me, but it surely made him stand out from the rest. Little did I know at the time, and for many years thereafter, what a profound influence he had on my life, my family and that northern Michigan community where my roots went so deep.

A.J. Haywood in the 1930's was an evangelist who crisscrossed northern Michigan, stopping in the rough and tumble lumbering communities to hold street meetings and when a school house was available, several weeks of services at a location. He came to Hillman, a village only a few miles west of Alpena, to preach, and people came to the Lord at his street meetings. He visited them in their homes and out in the fields where they were working

The Bentleys, a family of hillbillies recently emigrated from Kentucky, moonshiners running from the revenuers, were among those who found New Life as a result of his work, and were among the Hillman people who persuaded him to come to their community, ten miles west of Hillman, deep into the woods and hills– to preach there. He told them, "You find me a school house and I'll come." They did and Amos did.

The one-room school was near the little house in the deep woods where my mother was born and grew up. It was where later, my cousins, the grandchildren of those moonshiners, went to school, and

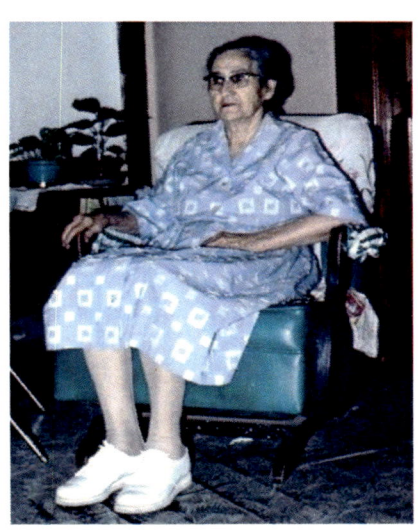

Birdella Bentley

where on one occasion I even visited school with them, for a day.

Every night for weeks, Amos Haywood preached to a full house with people hanging in the schoolhouse windows. Lives were changed forever. My grandmother, my mother and her numerous siblings attended those meetings, where many came to know the Lord.

The Kentucky hillbillies donated a corner of their property for a church and parsonage, a mile up the road from the school house. The little stone Pleasant Valley Free Methodist Church was built and assigned a pastor, to be attended by my ancestry and the community for a century or more. It is still going today.

Although my family moved south in the state when I was quite young, I often attended the church as a visitor when we visited the cousins or came north for the deer hunt. It was like my second home. And there was the day when I stood at the front with the other members of the Spring Arbor Quartet, singing "There waits for me a glad tomorrow," while Sister Bentley, ex-moonshiner with long black hair at the age of 70, ran the aisles, shouting and waving her hankie.

I have a prized possession, a little blue hard-cover of 200 yellowed pages, having neither copyright nor date, which is called "My Life Story." It was written by Amos Haywood. I don't remember how I came into possession of it, and I have wondered if perhaps I have the only copy still in existence. Imagine my surprise a few years ago, when I discovered the entire text of this book in a PDF file, on line. It is available at:

http://wesley.nnu.edu/wesleyctr/books/0801-0900/HDM0837.pdf .

Haywood's writing is an interesting read, quaint and sometimes amusing, but he was "salt of the earth," a courageous man who gave everything he had, and certainly made an indelible impact on our denomination and on the rugged people of the beautiful northern logging community that spawned my clan.

The Rise and Fall of [X] 8/31/2017
Assignment for ENL 453.01:
"History of the English Language"

An introductory note to this item: Massive kudos to anyone who reads to the end. Although that is not too likely, still I include the record here because I want to preserve it and the story behind it. This is the story.

I wrote this paper to fulfill a final requirement for completion of a grad course in history of the English language. Upon its completion I thought surely, I had hit the ball out of the park. Imagine my distress on that day when my paper was not returned with those of others in the class, but instead the prof asked me to meet him in his office following the session.

And there he leveled the accusation of plagiarism against me. I was floored. I explained my background, my familiarity with the sound from my four years of using Russian in the Air Force. I pointed out the extensive footnotes and bibliography concluding the assignment and insisted that there was no other source for the paper.

I suppose in a certain perverse manner of speaking, one might say the prof's accusation with such intense confidence amounts to praise of the highest order. I hold onto that, as the only reward I was to receive from the prof. Although he admitted that he could find nothing from which I might have plagiarized, nor any evidence of anything untoward, still he could not be convinced. After a meeting that lasted nearly an hour, he threw my paper at me with no score and no markings on it and excused me from his office. As well as I can recall, I was "awarded" a "C" for the course. What follows is the "plagiarized" paper.

Our objective is to chart the rise and fall of the voiceless velar spirant, [X] in the English language and in the Germanic which preceded. Strictly speaking, two voiceless spirants will be under discussion: a palatal spirant occurring after a front vowel, and a velar spirant which follows a back vowel sound, and since these differences were generally allophonic and since they result from the influence of the preceding vowel sound, we will group them together as one sound. (1)

The [X] did not exist in Indo-European, nor in fact did any spirant except the [S]. (2) There were, however, many occlusives, and it is in two of them that the [X] has its heritage. Those occlusives which were the forerunners of the [X] were both voiceless gutterals: the unaspirated [K] and the aspirated [KH]. (3)

As the Germanic dialects were developing, their consonantal structure underwent a radical change which we know as "Grimm's Law." That event, taking place over several centuries, included a shift from the occlusive [K] (except when it followed the [KH] or another occlusive,) to the occlusive [KH]. But since Germanic inherited a [KH] occlusive from Indo-European, the result was a merging of the [K] of most contexts with the occlusive [KH].

This merging was but an intermediate step in the consonantal change described by Grimm. The remaining step which probably occurred two or three centuries before Christ's birth, was the shift from a voiceless occlusive [KH] to the voiceless spirant [X]. (4) Such a change may have been made possible because the aspirated voiceless occlusives were not articulated very strongly; they therefore lost their occlusion and became spirants. (5)

Another explanation has been offered for that change; one which could have had a much greater impact. Very likely there was a neighboring group of people whose speech included the [X] spirant. These people adopted the Germanic dialect as their own language, but maintained that particular habit of articulation and thus influenced a change in the Germanic dialect. (6)

Whatever the causes, the fact is sure that the Indo-European [K] which had merged with the [KH] had been replaced with the unvoiced velar spirant by the first century, and the stage was now set for its gradual extinction over the next two thousand years.

The first step in that extinction of the [X] was made in company with several other sound changes in Germanic which collectively are known as Verner's Law. Verner stated that the voiceless fricatives, including [X] became voiced when they occurred between two voiced sounds, unless they immediately followed the main stress of the word. A modern English parallel might be seen in the first syllable of the words "exist" and "extra."

The second context from which the [X] was lost, was the initial location within the word. It was changed to either a breathing or a glottal spirant in Germanic, and by Middle English times even that breathing when preceding [l], [m], [n] or [w] had disappeared. (7)

Later in West Germanic a similar thing happened to medial [X] when located between two vowels, or between vowel and [l], [m], [n] or [r]. Again, it became a breathing spirant which disappeared early in Old English. (8)

Examples of this loss occurring between West Germanic and West Saxon are "slay" which changed from "slæXan" to "slæan" and "see" which changed from "seeXan" to "seean."

One other loss medially during the West Germanic period was from certain words in which [X] or [XS] became [KS]: "sieX" became "six," "oXa" became "ox," and "wax" from the word "weahson" with the spelling, [hs]. (9) A variation was that [XS] when following a consonant became simply [s], (10) as can be shown by "wXstan," "fruit," which is closely related to "weaXan."

The number of contexts in which [X] occurred in Primitive Germanic continued to decline through the Old English Period, with but a few reversals of the trend. But there were a few such instances which should be mentioned.

During the Old English Period, a terminal [K] frequently underwent a change to [X], which could be spelled either "h" or "g". (11)

Loan-words also served to augment the list of Germanic words with [Xt}, since that consonant cluster was substituted for a final [kt] in any Early Latin words which became a part of the English vocabulary. (12) An example of that substitution can be seen in "traht" from the Latin word "tractus," meaning "text."

By the beginning of the Middle English Period, [X] occurred chiefly in only two contexts: preceding "t" and terminally in a word. (13) It was not until nearly 1700 that it fell silent in its position before "t" (14) but we still preserve its memory whenever we write the "silent letters" of "brought," "sought," and "taught."

Several things happened to terminal [X] during the Middle English Period. In many words it was replaced with a high back vowel which was later lowered. (15) The word, "sorrow" is the result of such a change. It is from the Old English word, "sorh" which by Middle English times had become "sorwe."

Terminal [X] was often written "ch," due no doubt, to the example of some 13th century scribe of Norman descent. (16) In many words with that spelling, words such as "cough" and "laugh," the voiceless spirant shifted forward from velar or palatal position to become the labio-dental spirant, "f." (17)

In other cases such as the Old English "sooh" from which we have "shoe," and "saugh" which is an old "saw," the terminal [X] just fell silent.

The voiceless spirant, [X] is one of the few consonant sounds ever to disappear from our language, and only then after many centuries of tenaciousness. (18) Even today it is not quite possible to say it is extinct from the English language, for the person who listens to the dialectic speech of the Scotsman will find it lingering there, still.

A final note for anyone who actually reached this point: Forgive the absence of the footnotes and bibliography pages, as they are not only a pain to enter here, but are nearly undecipherable on my 40-year-old typewritten original. If anyone actually wants to see them, contact me and I will provide a copy of those originals. You may then try to read them to your heart's content.

Part 3. The Album

My Parents

Carol, Jimmy Painter

1. Mom and Dad holding Eric.

2. Dad with Eric and holding Deanne.

3. Marriage License.

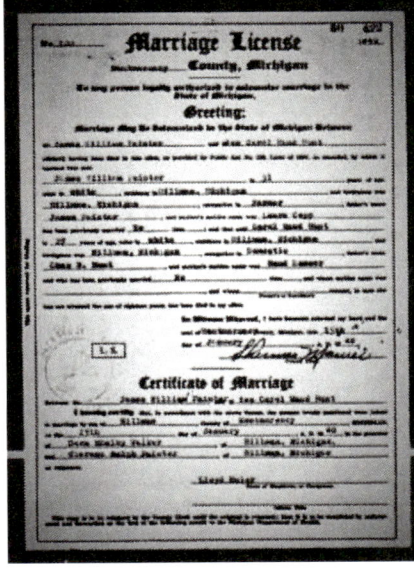

The Painter Pedigree

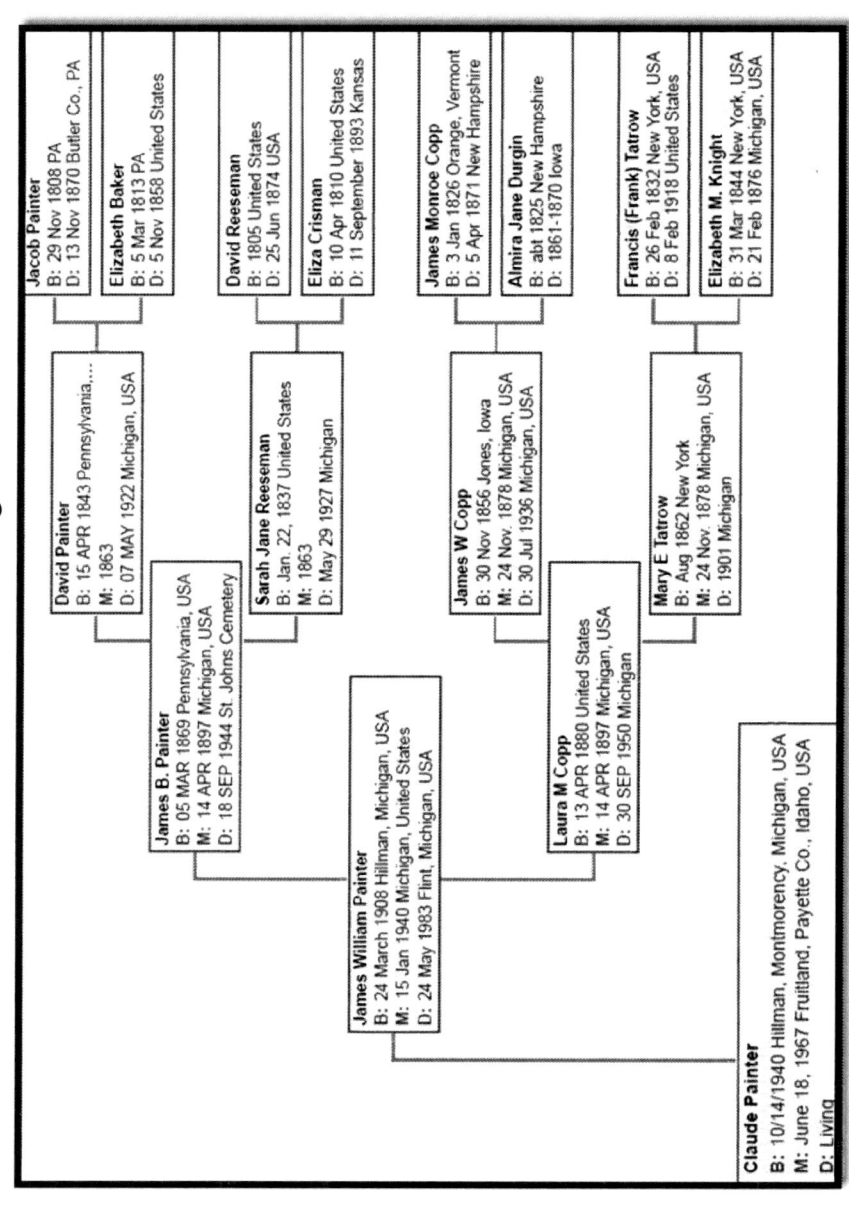

Claude Painter
B: 10/14/1940 Hillman, Montmorency, Michigan, USA
M: June 18, 1967 Fruitland, Payette Co., Idaho, USA
D: Living

James William Painter
B: 24 March 1908 Hillman, Michigan, USA
M: 15 Jan 1940 Michigan, United States
D: 24 May 1983 Flint, Michigan, USA

James B. Painter
B: 05 MAR 1869 Pennsylvania, USA
M: 14 APR 1897 Michigan, USA
D: 18 SEP 1944 St. Johns Cemetery

Laura M Copp
B: 13 APR 1880 United States
M: 14 APR 1897 Michigan, USA
D: 30 SEP 1950 Michigan

David Painter
B: 15 APR 1843 Pennsylvania,....
M: 1863
D: 07 MAY 1922 Michigan, USA

Sarah Jane Reeseman
B: Jan. 22, 1837 United States
M: 1863
D: May 29 1927 Michigan

James W Copp
B: 30 Nov 1856 Jones, Iowa
M: 24 Nov. 1878 Michigan, USA
D: 30 Jul 1936 Michigan, USA

Mary E Tatrow
B: Aug 1862 New York
M: 24 Nov. 1878 Michigan, USA
D: 1901 Michigan

Jacob Painter
B: 29 Nov 1808 PA
D: 13 Nov 1870 Butler Co., PA

Elizabeth Baker
B: 5 Mar 1813 PA
D: 5 Nov 1858 United States

David Reeseman
B: 1805 United States
D: 25 Jun 1874 USA

Eliza Crisman
B: 10 Apr 1810 United States
D: 11 September 1893 Kansas

James Monroe Copp
B: 3 Jan 1826 Orange, Vermont
D: 5 Apr 1871 New Hampshire

Almira Jane Durgin
B: abt 1825 New Hampshire
D: 1861-1870 Iowa

Francis (Frank) Tatrow
B: 26 Feb 1832 New York, USA
D: 8 Feb 1918 United States

Elizabeth M. Knight
B: 31 Mar 1844 New York, USA
D: 21 Feb 1876 Michigan, USA

The Hunt Pedigree

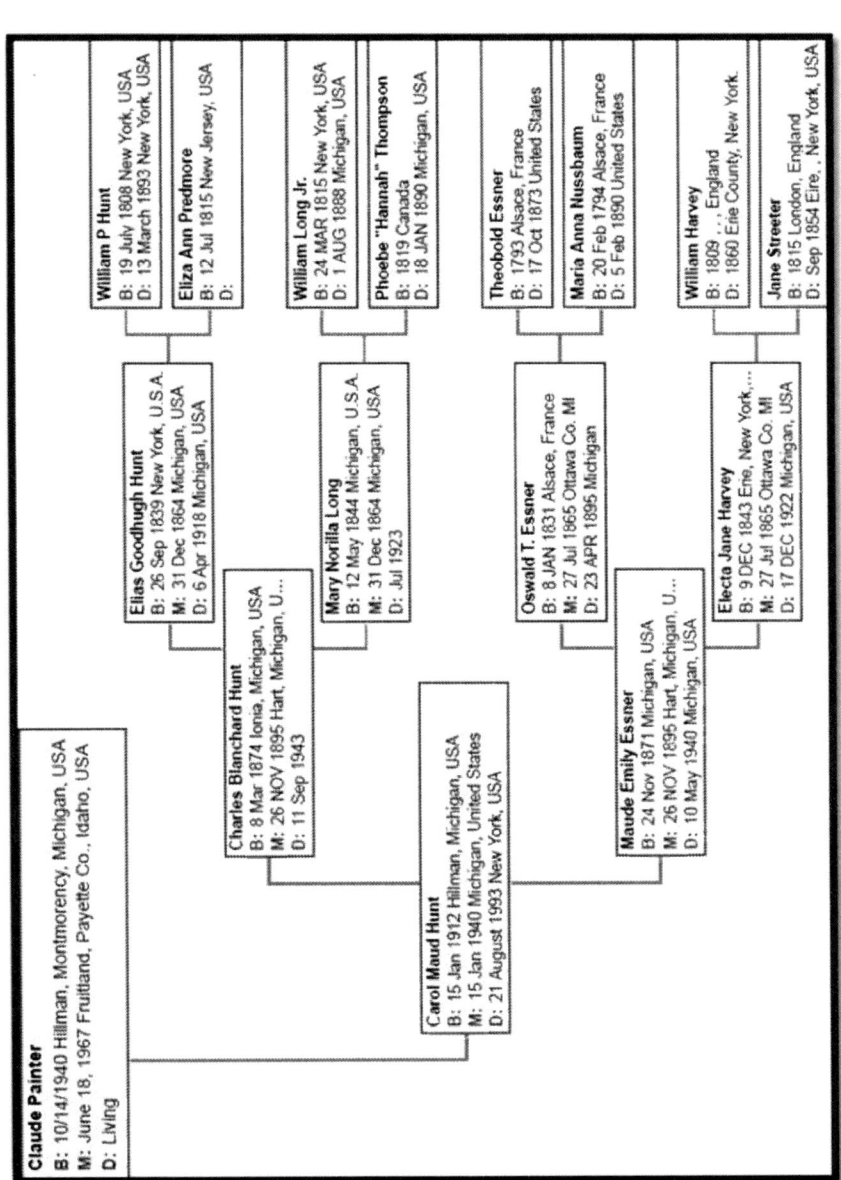

Claude Painter
B: 10/14/1940 Hillman, Montmorency, Michigan, USA
M: June 18, 1967 Fruitland, Payette Co., Idaho, USA
D: Living

Carol Maud Hunt
B: 15 Jan 1912 Hillman, Michigan, USA
M: 15 Jan 1940 Michigan, United States
D: 21 August 1993 New York, USA

Charles Blanchard Hunt
B: 8 Mar 1874 Ionia, Michigan, USA
M: 26 NOV 1895 Hart, Michigan, U...
D: 11 Sep 1943

Maude Emily Essner
B: 24 Nov 1871 Michigan, USA
M: 26 NOV 1895 Hart, Michigan, U...
D: 10 May 1940 Michigan, USA

Elias Goodhugh Hunt
B: 26 Sep 1839 New York, U.S.A.
M: 31 Dec 1864 Michigan, USA
D: 6 Apr 1918 Michigan, USA

Mary Norilla Long
B: 12 May 1844 Michigan, U.S.A.
M: 31 Dec 1864 Michigan, USA
D: Jul 1923

Oswald T. Essner
B: 8 JAN 1831 Alsace, France
M: 27 Jul 1865 Ottawa Co. MI
D: 23 APR 1895 Michigan

Electa Jane Harvey
B: 9 DEC 1843 Erie, New York,...
M: 27 Jul 1865 Ottawa Co. MI
D: 17 DEC 1922 Michigan, USA

William P Hunt
B: 19 July 1808 New York, USA
D: 13 March 1893 New York, USA

Eliza Ann Predmore
B: 12 Jul 1815 New Jersey, USA
D:

William Long Jr.
B: 24 MAR 1815 New York, USA
D: 1 AUG 1888 Michigan, USA

Phoebe "Hannah" Thompson
B: 1819 Canada
D: 18 JAN 1890 Michigan, USA

Theobold Essner
B: 1793 Alsace, France
D: 17 Oct 1873 United States

Maria Anna Nussbaum
B: 20 Feb 1794 Alsace, France
D: 5 Feb 1890 United States

William Harvey
B: 1809 ..., England
D: 1860 Erie County, New York.

Jane Streeter
B: 1815 London, England
D: Sep 1854 Eire,.. New York, USA

Maude

Maude Emily Essner stands between her brothers, Lewis on the left, and Albert. Seated is her mother, Electa Jane Harvey Essner and her father, Oswald Essner.

Below are the students of the one-room Crystal Lake School, Oceana County, Michigan in the 1880's. Wearing a plaid dress, my grandmother, Maud Essner, stands in the top row, second from the right.

Loggers

Loggers near Hilman, northern Michigan, about the year 1893. Second from left is my grandfather Charley Hunt at the age of 19, wrapped in a large piece of bark to hide a recent tear in his trousers. His brother, Sherman, is at the far right.

Charley Hunt, some years later, sits beside my Grandmother Maud. They had nine children, seven of which reached adulthood.

Maud passed in 1940 shortly before my birth, and Charley, two or three years later.

Carol, my mother, stands in the center behind her parents, Charley and Maud. They are flanked by her three brothers and three sisters, left to right, Ross, Ellis, Clyde, Arda, Mary, Bernice. Collectively this tribe of Hunts blessed me with cousins by the dozens, and with succeeding generations spanned the country, fulfilling with gusto the Biblical charge to populate the earth

My father's side, the Painter tribe, although numbering as many siblings as my mother's family, (Ethel, Jenny, Wes, Clarence, Lorne, Ray,) were abject failures in that regard, producing only one cousin that I am aware of, who like the rest, lived hard and died young.

Uncle Ray

This is the only picture I have of my father's siblings, his youngest brother, my Uncle Ray, here in his World War II uniform. Uncle Ray was my favorite of the bunch, perhaps because he was the only one that I ever really knew. It was not really a close-knit family.

242

Me 'n' Sis 'n' Grandpa Hunt –   Me 'n' my puppy

Me 'n' my school picture –   Me 'n' my first book

The home of my youth
in Durand.

Age 35 and still
growing up.

Joy Singers of the '70's

June 25, 1967
A day that shall live in infamy...

The Painter Family – Early 1970's

Esther and Claude, Soren on the left, Marcus on the right and Donita between them. Marcus and Soren suffered injuries at birth and were given to us on loan for only a few years.

Pretend Farmers

Above: The homemade barn and milk house which held as many as five dozen animals. Eric and Deanne "doing the chores."

Below: The "hay wagon" could haul up to two dozen bales at a time and the little goatherder could bottle-feed up to two dozen babies at a time.

Goats and Sheep

Nubian triplets:
Nubians: a floppy-eared breed of African lineage, high butterfat: 5 to 7%.

Alpine doe:
Esther has "set up" a young Alpine doe displaying its ribbon awarded at the county fair. Alpine and other European breeds have erect pointed ears.

Lincoln ram:
A black and silver colored sheep named Abe Ram Lincoln, and the all-time favorite of my flock. A docile English breed growing a beautiful silky fleece, a foot long, yearly.

Lincoln lamb:
Eric and Donita, with a half-lincoln lamb sired by Abe Ram Lincoln.

Smiles

Donita,
from her earliest days milked a good time for all it was worth.

If you must have a laugh, make it a memorable one.

Josh

Joshua Manning – Donita Painter Wedding Party

Chloe, Donita, Joshua

Eric

Eric, once my little boy, the best window breaker in New York State. Grew up overnight and suddenly became a handsome husband and a loving father. How did that happen?

Anya

Anya, Eric's child-bride who he hijacked from Russia, is pictured here with him and Santa, her boss, on her first job in the US. A lovely elf she was, speaking to the children with such a charming accent.

Anya was joined by Eric for a performance by the school she attended, Arts Triumphant, in Jacksonville. The photos show how remarkably Eric turned her world upside-down.

One Perfect Rose

Brian and Deanne Roes

I never shall forget
That perfect rose
He sent when first I met
That perfect Roes.

The perfect bait and switch
He now bestows,
Once, twice and then again,
That perfect Roes.

When will he substitute,
For Roes or rose -
That perfect limousine,
Do you suppose?

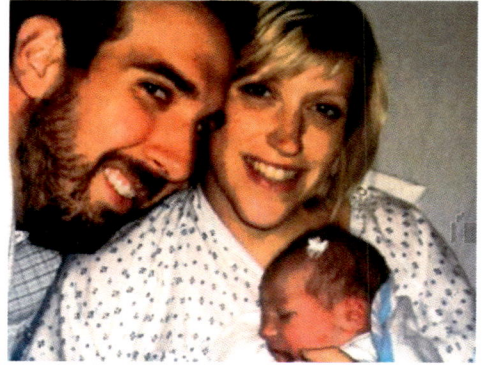

The Roes Kids

Alex, Brendan and Audrey Roes

Siblings and Cousins

Safiya, Audrey, Naya, Brendan, Nikita, Alex

Grandkids

Projects-1

What to do when retired? Anything creative, as you shall see.
Our Florida home with china cup-and-saucer pendant lighting.
Over the fireplace a mantle wired for lights above and below.

Projects-2

This photo album concludes by showing how I've kept entertained for the last decade – and expect to continue to be. Here you see a 30-foot walk and a step at the neighbor's house, a pantry on a laundry room wall, a home for 18 purple martin families, Esther's sewing table opened to display 120 spools of thread.

Projects-3

Nikita's closet needed a shelving and drawer system. A friend needed a play pen that would accept his child's mattress. The neighbors needed mailboxes with a whimsical flare. My front lawn needed a lamppost.

Projects-4

Made with PT decking:

dining room table on casters,

six foot Adirondack style bench sans cushions

Back patio,

12 by 20 feet,
625 pavers,
homespun with
Sakrete and hoe.

Projects-5

Pair of picnic tables made from PT decking, my own design: each will seat four, never a need to climb over benches.

Outer access to nest box on chicken coop, inclined floor, eggs roll to safety.

Shelving unit, horizontal pieces all made from recycled pallet wood.

Projects-6

A rare moment in this photo of a clean workbench in my shop.

My raised bed garden, 4 by 12 feet, 16 inches high and filled with topsoil. Timer on seepage hose under the soil, fencing underneath to repel moles, fabric over to deny the squirrels.

Projects-7

Fences. Lots of little fences.

A gateway arch for roses.

To walk off the patio and pick a fresh tangelo for breakfast or a lemon to squeeze into your tea, now that is the way to enjoy living in Florida.

A newly planted olive tree in the front yard. It joins the nectarines, the mango, the dozen citrus that surround the house. Living in an orchard is very cool.